Cherish

BCC PRESS

BY COMMON CONSENT PRESS is a non-profit publisher dedicated to producing affordable, high-quality books that help define and shape the Latter-day Saint experience. BCC Press publishes books that address all aspects of Mormon life. Our mission includes finding manuscripts that will contribute to the lives of thoughtful Latter-day Saints, mentoring authors and nurturing projects to completion, and distributing important books to the Mormon audience at the lowest possible cost.

Cherish

The Joy of Our Mother in Heaven

Curated by

Ashli Carnicelli
Trina Caudle
McArthur Krishna

Cherish: The Joy of Our Mother in Heaven
Copyright © 2023 by Ashli Carnicelli, Trina Caudle, and
  McArthur Krishna, editors

All rights reserved. Printed in the United States of America. No part of this book may be used or reproduced in any manner whatsoever without written permission except in the case of brief quotations embodied in critical articles or reviews.

For information contact
By Common Consent Press
4900 Penrose Dr.
Newburgh, IN 47630

Cover design: Kate Purcell
Book design: Andrew Heiss

www.bccpress.org
ISBN-13: 978-1-948218-87-0

10 9 8 7 6 5 4 3 2 1

Ashli Carnicelli

For my daughters—Isla Rose, Everly Belle, Adaline Mae, and Amelia Grace. May you always know who you are and whose you are. For Tony, for your love and your full support of the Catholic girl you married joining the Church. For my loving parents. For every precious person who added their hearts to this book. For my Savior, Jesus Christ, my All in All, who lovingly guides my safe return to my Heavenly Parents.

Trina Caudle

For Adam, Aster, Marnie, Jenna, Tenley, and Josie, my reason for everything I do. For my parents, who taught me to always follow the Lord, especially when He leads me into the unexpected. "It's an adventure!"

McArthur Krishna

For sisterhood sanity

Contents

	An Explanation of our Hearts	ix
	Following the Savior	1
1.	Beloved Spirit Children	27
2.	Cherished and Distinctive Doctrine	65
3.	A Mother There	107
4.	Side By Side	143
5.	Divine Nature and Destiny	179
6.	Work Together	219
7.	Designers of the Divine Plan	247
8.	Influences From Beyond	275
9.	Connection	315
10.	Eternal Prototype	345
11.	Sacred Knowledge	381
12.	Highest Aspiration	423
	A Celebration of Joy	453
	Contributors	479
	References	487

An Explanation of our Hearts

∽

People always wonder how a book like this comes to be . . .

McARTHUR: I have spoken of Heavenly Mother to thousands of women. Every single time, I see the Spirit move women with such POWER. Women get lit on fire! I was thinking about what Mother in Heaven means to every single person, and I wanted to hear their voices.

ASHLI: I had a project on my heart. I felt inspired to create a book of poetry about Heavenly Mother that included the stunning artwork of Latter-day Saints who are inspired by this doctrine, a sort of "Grown-Up Girl's Guide to Heavenly Mother." For months, the Spirit prompted me to reach out to McArthur and I finally sent her a message. We spoke on the phone and gave ourselves twenty-four hours to pray about it. I fasted and went to the temple. As I entered the Celestial room and sat down to pray, the revelation came. "YES, Ashli! This joyful doctrine is true. This is OUR work. Write the book. Just make sure you are still pointing people to Christ." I called McArthur from the car and shared this revelation. She went quiet for a few moments, then replied, "Wow. I got the same revelation. Let's get to work!"

TRINA: I saw a social media post from McArthur and Ashli asking for contributions for a new Heavenly Mother book, and immediately wanted to be part of the project. I'm a writer and editor so that's a typical reaction to seeing book proposals. But this time felt different. It was a prompting I've had before: the Spirit points and says, "There. Go. Right now." And I am restless until I follow through. I'm not a poet or an artist, but I can organize the heck out of manuscripts. Within minutes, I sent McArthur a message. In a few more minutes, my phone rang and that was that.

Joined together, we asked: What does Heavenly Mother mean to each of us? What does Heavenly Mother mean to others?

This is not a book of doctrine. This is not a book of speculation. This is not a book intended to answer all, or any, spiritual questions.

This is a book of musings of the soul. Everyone was welcome to contribute. Every person is a beloved child of Heavenly Mother and Father, and that means something different to each of us! The mediums of poetry and art are just two of many ways for us to communicate spiritually. If our Heavenly Parents are infinite beings, then there are infinite touch points to honor Them.

We organized the contributions around the Gospel Topics Essay "Mother in Heaven," to support study of that vital document. We also included scriptures and quotes from prophets and other Church leaders to help guide us. The Church is the "scaffolding" to our faith, but we want to be clear that the vignettes are personal.

We hope the offerings within these pages bring joy to your soul. You have a Mother in Heaven!

INTRODUCTION

Following the Savior

"My dear brothers and sisters, **Jesus Christ** invites us to take **the covenant path back home to our Heavenly Parents** and be with those we love. He invites us to 'Come, follow me.'"

President Russell M. Nelson[1]

Hope in Oneness

I and my Father are one, Christ says.
The Father and the Mother,
in perfect equal partnership,
Must also be One.
If I become one with Christ,
I can also be one with
My Mother and my Father.

                    Angela Ricks

Joy

Isn't this joyous! We have this earth life to develop our souls so we can return to live in harmony with our Parents. The gifts that They have in store for us—eternal life, eternal families, exaltation—these alone are more than I can comprehend. However, it's easy to get discouraged along the way. Thankfully, our Parents have provided help for the journey. Our most vital help is our Brother, Jesus Christ, and His atonement. Christ makes our celestial reunion and living in the presence of our Heavenly Parents possible. That truth fills me to overflowing with love and gratitude for the Savior!

McArthur Krishna

Who We Are and Where We Are

We have a Heavenly Mother. We were created in Her image. She is our eternal prototype. She loves us. She cares about our salvation and our eternal progression. She works together with Heavenly Father for our salvation.

Let those truths sink in. How does your life change living from those truths? How do you see yourself differently? How do you see others differently?

One of my close friends is a preschool teacher. She recalled a time when one of her students was getting out of the car to come to school. The little girl exclaimed, "I know who I am and I know where I am!" Do we know who we are? Do we know where we are? I would add: do we know *whose* we are? I believe with this doctrine, we answer those most essential questions. We know who we are. We know where we are. We know where we are headed.

Ashli Carnicelli

We are beloved spirit sons and daughters of heavenly parents, with a divine nature and destiny. Our Savior, Jesus Christ, loved us enough to give His life for us. His Atonement provides the way for us to progress on the path to our heavenly home, through sacred priesthood ordinances and covenants.

Sister Carole M. Stephens, counselor in Relief Society general presidency, 2012-2017[2]

And

I love my dad AND my mom. I love my three brothers AND my four sisters. I love their spouses AND their children. I love my spouse AND my children. I love more friends than I can name. I love our Heavenly Father AND our Heavenly Mother AND our Brother Jesus Christ.

Love is not a zero sum game in which we must take love from one person to give it to another. Love grows exponentially and eternally—the more you give away, the more you have. We have love, so we share love, so we have more love, until we become love.

Trina Caudle

She

Mindy Sebastian

Nursing

She was my first fount of living water
My Savior, my second
How blessed to know that They never run dry

Autumn Nelson

"You are unique, each with your own gifts and experiences yet alike in a very important and eternal way. You are literally the spirit daughters of Heavenly Parents, and nothing can separate you from Their love and the love of your Savior."

President Bonnie H. Cordon,
Young Women general president,
2018-present[5]

Where Are We Going?

If we follow Christ, He leads to our Parents.

McArthur Krishna

My Mother's Love

My Mother's love
fills me with joy
as I feel Her
wrapping me up
with all of Her favorite things—
with Hope
with Love
with Encouragement
with the Fruits of the Spirit
with Wisdom
with Peace
with Confidence
Each a fragrant bud
upon a crown of flowers
She places on my head
Each time that I repent
and turn to Her Son.
No effort goes unnoticed
No failure forever
No imperfection that can't be made perfect

through Him.
Each day
I labor beside Her
Pruning this small quiver
of tiny Queens
that She helped knit together
in my womb
That He protected
coming into the world.
There isn't anything
about every day
that is ordinary
Every moment
Truly is
A miracle
It all starts and ends
and starts again
From my Mother's Love.

        Ashli Carnicelli

Borne

Surely He has borne our grief.
Who better than my Mother knows,
How He must be feeling; felt,
For did She not Herself bear all?

Jessica Burdette

"It doesn't take from our worship of the Eternal Father to adore our Eternal Mother, any more than it diminishes the love we bear our earthly fathers, to include our earthly mothers in our affections.... We honor woman when we acknowledge Godhood in her eternal prototype."

Elder Rudger Clawson[4]

Ever Present

She is there.
Always has been.
In the flowers I see passing
On the side of the road
Beautifying the earth.

She is there.
Always has been.
Her shadow comforts me
As the sun sets while I
Ache for perfection.

She is here.
In the present.
As I wrap my arms
Around my mournful child
And love her whole.

She is here.
Ever present.
As she wraps Her perfect arms
Around Her mournful child
And guides me home.

Pointing to Her Son.

Who is here.
Ever present.
Paving the way through
Valleys of hardship and
Mountains of mortality.
Loving me whole.
Guiding me home.
To Them.

Anonymous

"Whereby are given unto us exceeding great and precious promises: that by these ye might be partakers of the divine nature."

2 Peter 1:4

My First Vision

Come to think of it
I do remember the first time I knew Mother
as clear as a Spring morning
She came to me in my ponderings
Her glory defied all description
and was above the brightness of the sun
She spake to me,
Calling me by name and said
Woman, (the name many of us bear)
This is my beloved song
Sing it.

Olivia Flinders

Heavenly Mother is Essential

Heavenly Mother IS essential to the plan. She and Heavenly Father together are our end goal. Returning back to Her and Heavenly Father's presence is an essential part of the plan, and Christ's greatest concern as our Advocate and as our Redeemer. Christ redeems us from our sins through His Atonement. He saves us from spiritual death and offers us eternal life. Part of that eternal life is being worthy of existing in Their presence. All of this is described in Alma 42—the plan of happiness, our redemption, and our resurrection—I testify that these things are true.

Ashli Carnicelli

Believe Christ

～

As a young teenager I came across a small book in my dad's office called "Believing Christ" by Stephen E. Robinson. In this book, Robinson reframes faith in Christ, saying:

> "To have faith in Jesus Christ is not merely to believe that he is who he says he is. It is not merely to believe *in* Christ; we must also *believe* Christ."

He shares various examples of people who claimed they believed in Christ, but still felt that they themselves were inadequate or unworthy, either of a mortal task or of eternal life altogether. He says, "All of these are variations on the same theme: 'I do not believe Christ can do what He claims. I have no faith in His ability to exalt me.'"

To believe Christ, then, requires that I believe that Christ's promises of redemption and exaltation apply to *me*.

At times in my life, as I waded the depths

of doctrinal questions about my eternal destiny as a woman, the cultural misconceptions about my Heavenly Mother—my eternal prototype—built an image of eternal womanhood as withdrawn, silent, ignored, unimportant, and altogether un-exalted.

If my eternal prototype is in any way less—less glorious, less important, less involved, less powerful, less perfect—than our living, omnipotent, perfect Heavenly Father. . . . If somehow my eternal destiny is inherently *un-exalted* (only because of my gender!), then the Savior's promises must not apply to me!

With this limited vision of my Heavenly Mother, I have a very hard time truly believing that all of Christ's promises apply to me, a woman created in the image of my Heavenly Mother.

On the other hand, as I shed the cultural misconceptions and fully embrace truths found in scriptural and prophetic teachings about Her—Her exalted and glorious status, Her role in the eternal plan, Her strength and wisdom, and Her place as co-creator and co-equal with the Father—I can *fully believe* Christ.

My relationship with and trust in the Savior has deepened exponentially as I have developed an understanding of our Heavenly Mother's perfect unity and equality with our loving Heavenly Father. I am more resolved to follow Christ, more committed to His gospel, and more able to exercise wholehearted faith in Him.

Because of my knowledge and testimony of Heavenly Mother, I can unreservedly *believe* Christ.

Alynne Scirkovich

Come and Partake

> "Surely the thing God enjoys most about being God is the thrill of being merciful, especially to those who don't expect it and often feel they don't deserve it."
> —Elder Jeffrey R. Holland[5]

Our Heavenly Mother's invitation matches our Heavenly Father's, inviting all of Her children to come and partake of the love and mercy of God. We will make mistakes, we will fall, and She will be there encouraging us to get back up and try again until we eventually reach Her outstretched arms and partake of the love of perfect Heavenly Parents. They love us beyond our ability to comprehend. Their invitation is united in purpose, to encourage us to do good and bring us all back home.

Kristina A. Bishoff

"Jesus answered them, Is it not written in your law, I said, ye are gods?"

John 10:34

1
Beloved Spirit Children

"The Church of Jesus Christ of Latter-day Saints teaches that all human beings, male and female, are **beloved spirit children** of heavenly parents, a Heavenly Father and a Heavenly Mother."

Mother in Heaven essay, paragraph 1

Identity

Knowing my identity as a child of God—that I am a daughter of Heavenly Mother—changes EVERYTHING. It has changed how I carry myself in the world and how I view others. Knowing that I am both made in Her image and destined to become like Her has changed my decisions, how I spend my time, what I value, and my relationships.

Ashli Carnicelli

"I testify there is no greater goal in mortality than to live eternally with our Heavenly Parents and our beloved Savior, the Lord Jesus Christ. But it is more than just our goal—it is also Their goal. They have a perfect love for us, more powerful than we can even begin to comprehend. They are totally, completely, eternally aligned with us. We are Their work. Our glory is Their glory. More than anything else, They want us to come home—to return and receive eternal happiness in Their presence."

Elder M. Russell Ballard[6]

"For behold, this is my work and my glory—to bring to pass the immortality and eternal life of man."

Moses 1:39

We Are Their Work and Their Glory

Can you even imagine what that means? I can't. I try. But the sheer immensity of that overwhelms me. Instead of trying to comprehend, now I just try to swaddle myself and rest in it.

McArthur Krishna

Remember, Little One

Remember, little one: Not so long ago
Heavenly parents dear held you oh so close.
Now today, here you are, wonderfully alive.
In your eyes, shining still, Heaven's light abides.
Oh tell me, little one, of our home above,
For your veil is so thin. Tell me of Their love.

Remember, little one, prairies, towns, and pines.
Can we see here on earth such a view divine?
And the sky, when night falls, is it pink or gray?
Does the sun yield to snow, does it follow rain?
Draw for me, little one, scenes of fields so bright.
Sing to me melodies of that world tonight.

Cherish

Remember, little one: When it all began,
We were friends, very best, playing hand in hand.
Then one day, joyfully, we did choose, did we,
The great plan of our Lord, life with agency.
That night then, little one, we promised in love
And in faith to again reunite above.

Marie Françoise Euvrard

Included in the French language hymnbook of the
Church of Jesus Christ of Latter-day Saints

Translated into English by Britt Manjarrez

Supreme Beings

The most Supreme Beings of the universe are there to help us. Really? Believe it. Even if you don't want to, even if you doubt, even if it seems it can't possibly be true . . . try. Let it sink into your soul.

McArthur Krishna

"The Spirit itself beareth witness with our spirit, that we are the children of God: And if children, then heirs; heirs of God, and joint-heirs with Christ; if so be that we suffer with him, that we may be also glorified together."

Romans 8:16-17

Freckles

"Mom, you are beautiful!"
Her 7-year-old toothless grin trips on the "r" in the phrase
She's joined me in the bathroom where hairspray and makeup litter the counter
I have plucked and preened each stray hair
Gray hairs
Covered my freckles in colors and creams
Her freckled cheeks are pink from cartwheeling into the room
She never walks anymore
Her wildness shows in her tangled hair—lighter than mine
And I am overcome with her beauty
Long, dark eyelashes frame her sparkling green eyes
Busy hands still have glitter on them from creating at the kitchen table

Her long legs hugged by bright green leaf-covered leggings
I am enamored with her creativity and energy and soul
I wonder if this is how my Heavenly Mother takes me in at the end of the day
Softly loving the details She recognizes in me
Pointing them out to her Husband
She has your kindness
She has my temper
She has your fire
She has my stillness
These details bring Them joy
For They created them
They created me

Kristin Miller

"All men and women are in the similitude of the universal Father and Mother and are literally the sons and daughters of Deity."

First Presidency, 1909[7]

Soul Balm

No matter where we come from and who our earthly parents are, we are loved perfectly by our Heavenly Parents. How does it feel to be *beloved*? You are ALWAYS loved. When we think the demands of life are too much for us, isn't it a lovely balm to remember that They are on our team?

McArthur Krishna

I Have A Mother

I have a Father
I have a Mother
And I can feel her
Close around me

I hear her whispers
In gentle breezes
I hear her calling me
She heals me

I see her beauty
All surrounding me
I feel her warmth
And love abounding

Krystal Richey Barnes

Her House

Do you think She
ever walks the white halls of
Her house
and touches every lace altar
every stained glass window
every foggy veil
and hopes that one of Her
children will see Her prints glisten?
A memory of Her—
an emblem of her—
an evidence beyond reason.

Olivia Flinders

"You have light because you are literally spirit daughters of Deity, 'offspring of exalted parents' with a divine nature and an eternal destiny. You received your first lessons in the world of spirits from your heavenly parents."

President Julie B. Beck, counselor in Young Women general presidency, 2002-07; Relief Society general president, 2007-12[8]

My Mother's Eyes

If one day I stare
Into Her eyes,
Will I be surprised to find
The similarities between
Her eyes and mine?

In the mirror I see
Eyes in search of Her.
Will one day I see
Her eyes in search of me?

Ashley Lauren Workman

Psalm to the Seamstress

∽

weave me, dear Mother, into your spirit and skin

embroider in my body your words of unfailing love

with deft fingers at the spindle of my heart spin my spirit into song

pull my threads taut, order my fraying fragments together

braid my unruly strings into strength and command creation from my chaos

knit your wisdom across my temple

stitch your intuition into my sight

bind your love into my breath

veil me in your power, like a little girl playing dress-up in her mother's closet

putting her too-small feet into the too-big
   shoe, vanishing under the folds of a dress
   in a size she has yet to grow into

my cloth is yours
take my modest offering for your tapestry
   and swathe me deep into the fabric of
   your creation
let me, dear Mother, be woven into your womb
   and the palms of your hands and your
   heart and eyes and mind
so close, dear Mother, that you may never be
   more than a heartbeat away
so close, dear Mother, that every needle-prick
   in my tissue may resound in witness of you

Autumn Nelson

Mother God

Jessie Payne

She's Like Her Son

I think that Heavenly Mother looks for those who are in the margins. I think She listens and learns. I think that like Her Son, Jesus Christ, Her bowels are filled with mercy for us. I think She tries to help us when we have done all that we can and still feel like we are not enough. I think She weeps for Her children who feel like they don't fit the mold, and offers Her unfailing love—just like the Savior did during His earthly ministry.

Ashli Carnicelli

Ima

In the Garden, our Brother cried for *Abba*.
On the Cross, He looked down at Mary
and in her blazing eyes
He recognized Mother—
Her strength,
Her support,
Her love—
radiant in each daughter
who turns to Her light.
He didn't call out for *Ima*.
He felt Her presence there.

Lorren Lemmons

"The plan teaches that all who have or will live on earth are the spirit children of heavenly parents. We lived with them before coming to this earth to receive our bodies of flesh and bone."

Elder M. Russell Ballard[9]

Madeleine Wells

It is not just Heavenly Father that will love us forever. Heavenly Mother will love us forever too. Their love never ends.

Zara Krishna, age 6

Who But a Mother?

Who but a mother recognizes the beautiful diversity and divinity of her LGBTQ child?

Who has eyes that see meaning and possibilities where others see incongruity?

Whose inviolable heartstrings feel a child's joy and pain more acutely than her own?

Who whispers words of wisdom to unlock fears and communicate confidence to blaze trails, knowing so many more will follow?

Who loves with such power she illuminates the way back home?

Who but a mother?

Who but the Mother?

Allison Dayton

Hear Him

As we studied the First Vision in a recent class, I found myself wondering if Heavenly Mother was there. I wondered what She would have said.

I thought of how my Heavenly Mother can speak to me. I hear Her voice in the music that I sing, in the rustling of leaves in the fall, and flowing streams. She reminds me that She loves me and that I matter. She reminds me of my potential. Just like the Father, She says, "This is My Beloved Son. Hear Him!" In all things, She points me to my Savior and inspires me to be more like Him.

Malinda Wagstaff

Sacred Sway

∽

My baby will not sleep tonight
She is ill and only rests in my arms
I am rocking, rocking, rocking and I am tired
My eyes are heavy and my arms are sore
And still I sway
For a moment I wish this moment away
That she would sleep and that I could sleep
But then I catch sights of my shadow on the walls
Performing that sacred sway
That ancient dance of comfort
And sometimes of sacrifice
And I find myself thinking of Her
I am sure She rocked us to sleep before we came to this earth
Does She ever wish she could still do it now?
Late at night when we are restless or wrestling

Does She wish She could hold us in Her arms
 and lull us gently back
into peace?
And then the tide came to my mind
The rising and falling of the ocean in a rhythmic
 pattern
And the perfect breeze that sways the treetops
Back and forth
Back and forth
Back and forth
On a summer's day
And the rolling of the moon and the sun
 around and around
And I realized
She does

Alyssa Wilkinson

"Brothers and sisters, we are eternal beings, without beginning and without end. We have always existed. We are the literal spirit children of divine, immortal, and omnipotent Heavenly Parents!"

Elder Dieter F. Uchtdorf[10]

Coming

I am yours,
Never alone.
Through my doors,
Coming home.

You are mine,
Always near.
Through time,
Becoming clear.

We are one,
Your love in me.
My heart finds yours,
And then I see.

I'll always seek you,
I feel your pull.
I know I'll meet you.
Then I'll be whole.

Maddie Daetwyler

As I Have Loved You

How do I love thee?
You're perfect, my child.
You fill me, delight me
The day shines more brightly
I can't picture life without you.

How does She love me?
"You're perfect, my child.
You fill me, delight me
The day shines more brightly
I can't picture life without you."

Jessica Burdette

I Cherish You

Rowan Li Forsyth

Just Be

Hustle, hustle for value and worth
out there, somewhere after a checklist or goal.
It's an illusion, you know.
Checkmarks aren't gods.
Why did I chase them so hard?

Unconditional, expansive love from Mother
Is setting my record straight.
Just be, She whispers.
Really, you want me to rest?

Long exhale, ungripped hands,
Relief in Her presence.
To Her I am beloved, cherished, adored
With scars, foibles, quirks.

Cherish

Like my gushing love for my babies,
No checklist is required of them
to earn value, worth, love from me.
It's present, expansive, overflowing.
I can't help myself.

With Her, no need to hustle, hustle for value
 and worth.
I am filled.

Just be.

Becky Edwards

Down

I think that Mother looks down
Through the stars
Through the firmament
And through the clouds to look
Upon Her creation.

I think She whispers,
"I love you.
You are good.
You are mine."

I think I feel Her say it.

Lee Correia

"I want to talk about [being] a daughter. This means who I am in relation to deity. I have Divine Parents and that means that I belong to their household of God. I have rights and privileges and blessings that are associated with being their child. . . . They are teaching me and I can seek and they promise that I will find. I can ask and they promise, 'You will receive.' I am a daughter and I am hungry for knowledge and wisdom and information and progression."

Sister Sharon Eubank,
counselor in Relief Society
general presidency, 2017-22[11]

Looking Around

It's amazing to see what you can find if you
    only look for it.
Here She is. There She is.
That's my Mama

Autumn Nelson

2

Cherished and Distinctive Doctrine

"The **doctrine** of a Heavenly Mother is a **cherished and distinctive** belief among Latter-day Saints."

Mother in Heaven essay, paragraph 1

Definitions

Cherish: to hold dear, to care deeply, to treasure, to treat with affection and tenderness, to feel or show great love.

> "We were gentle among you, even as a nurse cherisheth her children: So being affectionately desirous of you, we were willing to have imparted unto you, not the gospel of God only, but also our own souls, because ye were dear unto us."
> —1 Thessalonians 2:7-8

Distinctive: a characteristic that makes a person or thing different from others in a way that is easy to notice, appealing or interesting because of its unique or special qualities.

Trina Caudle

Cherish

I love the scripture that talks about what happens when the world comes to know the works of God—the morning stars sing together and children of God shout for joy. That is quite a celebration! I cherish the gift of my body, so I dance. I cherish the gift of my agency, so I explore. I cherish the gift of the Savior, so I repent. If we want to truly honor our belief in Heavenly Mother, how do we apply it to our lives?

McArthur Krishna

A Doctrine of Joy

As a convert to The Church of Jesus Christ of Latter-day Saints, the Book of Mormon gives me SO much joy with the fulness of the gospel. The doctrine of Heavenly Mother, also unique to this church, is a doctrine of joy for women and men alike.

Ashli Carnicelli

The Veil is Beginning to Burst

Rose Datoc Dall

"We have heavenly parents, a father and a mother. The doctrine of a Heavenly Mother comes by revelation and is a distinctive belief among Latter-day Saints."

Elder Dale G. Renlund[12]

Restoration

~

Through the direction of the Lord, Joseph Smith restored the doctrine of Heavenly Mother and began the process of restoring us to Her.

Though Joseph did not publicly teach about Heavenly Mother, some of his close associates, including Zina D. Huntington, bore record that he personally taught them about Her in Nauvoo.

In 1839, after losing her mother to cholera, Zina asked Joseph, *"Will I know my mother as my mother when I get over on the Other Side?"*

"Certainly you will," was the instant reply of the Prophet. *"More than that, you will meet and become acquainted with your eternal Mother, the wife of your Father in Heaven."*[13]

I believe that bringing knowledge of Heavenly Mother to the world is a crucial aspect of the Restoration and of the salvation of all humankind. It is essential to restoring women and men to their proper relationship—one of complementary, equal partnership in unity with one another. The Restoration is ongoing, and I believe more will be revealed about our Heavenly Mother in order to restore us to our heavenly home.

Aspen Moore

Seeking

If we can study the scriptures to learn more about Heavenly Mother and pray just like in Moroni—"pray to know if these things are NOT true"—if I'm going to approach something as holy as Heavenly Mother, this is how I'm going to pray as I study! I have hope that this doctrine is true. I'm going into it with that expectation as I ponder and ask.

Shima Baughman

A Psalm for Nature's Tabernacle

∽

If I could see the rings
Of the great Tree of Life
Perhaps I could behold the aging
And wisdom of the Wife.

If my fingers could stroke
Over an eternity of Her,
Marked in the oak,
The moments that were;

Eons would be in Her wooden halos.
A journal of the trees;
Joys and sorrows,
Sacrifice, to bring me to my knees.

I'd pass my trembling fingers
O'er the lessons learned.
These patterns bearing Her words
And the Divinity She's earned.

This Sacred Tree would tell scripture
Of a wise heart that knew:
Though Her Son bled from every pore,
That we needed Him too.

Her rings would tell me stories
Of Her work
Of Her Glory.

Though She is not truly wooden
I do like to ponder in earth's tabernacle of trees.

Though She is in my own image
I do long to see Her rings.

Ashley Lauren Workman

Her

Perhaps She is the feeling of warm sunshine
   on bare skin
my favorite feeling

And perhaps when I sit in the window light
and write poems
She is wrapped around me
and Her light floods my vision
the warm sun
whispering what to write
to love Her into our world.

        Olivia Flinders

"If thou shalt ask, thou shalt receive revelation upon revelation, knowledge upon knowledge, that thou mayest know the mysteries and peaceable things—that which bringeth joy, that which bringeth life eternal."

D&C 42:61

Divine Dignity

The world asks us to seek out our self-esteem through what we do and what we achieve. Knowing the doctrine of Heavenly Mother has made me realize that I can instead experience a sense of divine dignity because of who I am, and whose I am. This sense of self-esteem is not centered around self at all—instead, it is centered around the plan of happiness, with Jesus Christ at the very core. While what I choose to do is important, my worth doesn't change.

Ashli Carnicelli

Blessed Name of Mother

∾

"And what is there in the natural man or woman that revolts at the idea of a Heavenly Mother? The sublime attributes which are ascribed to Deity are just those which have immortalized the name of mother. Fatherhood and motherhood are co-equal in sacred office on earth, but childhood wants mother. That's why babes delight to hear of the Heavenly Mother. . . .

"An unknown author has said, 'Not only from the mouths of babes and sucklings has the cry gone forth for a Mother in heaven. Men, strong and brave, have yearned to adore her. The heart of man craves this faith and has from time immemorial demanded the deification of woman.' It doesn't take from our worship of the Eternal Father, to adore our Eternal Mother, any more than it diminishes the love we bear our earthly fathers, to include our earthly mothers in our affections, in fact, the love of one is a complement of our love for the other. We honor woman when we ackno[w]ledge Godhood in her eternal Prototype. And, man may never hope to reach the high destiny marked out for him by the Savior in these encouraging [w]ords: 'Be ye perfect, even as your Father which is in heaven is perfect,' without woman by his side; for 'neither is the man without the woman, neither the woman without the man, in the Lord.' Then let us respond to the lofty theme of George Griffith Fetter:

"The noblest thoughts my soul can claim.
The holiest words my tongue can frame,
Unworthy are to praise the name
More sacred than all other.
An infant, when her love first came —
A man, I find it just the same;
Reverently I breathe her name,
The [B]lessed name of mother!"

Elder Rudger Clawson[14]

Young Women Theme

~

> "I am a beloved daughter of Heavenly Parents, with a divine nature and eternal destiny."

The opening of the Young Women Theme revised in 2019 is profound and powerful. Consider the deep meaning of these words and the effect they will have on the young women of the Church who grow up reciting them every week. Think of what it would have meant to you as a young woman or Primary-aged girl to know you had a Heavenly Mother and a Heavenly Father who both knew you individually, who loved you unconditionally, and were present in your life.

Take a few moments today to write a note to a young woman or young girl in your life—either in your family or your ward or a class that you teach—to share with her the love of Heavenly Mother and Heavenly Father. Bear your testimony of Their love for all of Their children. Share how you have felt that love in your own life.

Rebecca Young

Represents

Nature tender mild
Milky cottonwood seeds dust
Close to heaven grand

Represents all love
Gentle breeze carries the show
Winter scenes, summer

Heaven's gentle grace
Represents loving ally
Mother, tender source.

April Green

Along Those Lines

I didn't have a daughter. Lots of little boys came to me from heaven, but sometimes I feel like I am the last girl in my line.

Except, I'm connected to my grandmas. They raise my babies with me in the night, and see my tears when I'm alone. I knead one's bread, play the other's piano.

And there are future daughters I'll be connected to.

Because we all came from Her. And we're all helping each other find Her, and Home.

Maddie Daetwyler

Pearl of Greatest Price

Souls search
far and wide
for the jewel above any treasure
they traverse oceans
deserts
mountain tips and
dark caves
digging into the earth
breaking every clam for
a glimpse of the precious.

Just when they think
they've seen every priceless stone
and know all the secrets of the kingdom
they stand all amazed at

the image of a woman with
lustrous flesh
slightly iridescent
The Holy She
The Pearl of Greatest Price
not inside a clam or a cave
rather
upward in the sky and
in front of their eyes.

                Olivia Flinders

She Will

One night like a child
I told Mommy,
I'm scared of the
dark in my room.
She said, I know,
softly, like the kind of
soft God-Mother
She is.

The next night, I told
Her, I'm more
scared of the
dark in my heart.
She said, I know.

Cherish

The last night, I told
Her, I'm most
scared of the
dark in my life.
She said, I know.

I begged Her, Stay
with me. Hold my
hand until I fall
asleep. Let me hear
Your voice.
She said, I will.

    Rachel Hunt Steenblik

Holy Stories

Part of my work includes helping women writers craft their stories. Each woman's story is holy, set apart for a sacred purpose. Women I work with see the divine design of their lives. They embody Orson F. Whitney's claim that all we endure in this earthly life—the joy and pain alike—can make us "more like our Father and Mother in heaven."[15] As these women writers bravely share their life-learned wisdom, they invite other sisters to experience a closer relationship with our Savior. How can your unique life experiences be used to strengthen other women in becoming more like our Mother in Heaven?

Christie Gardiner

Why My Heart Sings

I hear my heart sing—
Feel it beat in my chest,
Like a lost child in the arms of a stranger,
Seeing their mother across the room.
Frantic to reach joy
In the safety and discovery that is her.

But who is she?
Who calls my name with the familiar tone,
The sound and scent of home.
Who strokes my hair when sleep eludes me,
And the world is cruel.

Who whispers words of comfort
Then feeds my soul my favorite foods
Just because I was hungry
And I asked.

She is big when I am small
Rocking me in the rocking chair
Sharing story after story—

Some new.
Some old.
And smiling as I add another book to the pile.

I felt her love before I knew her name—
Even now she is simply called
"Mother"
She is me.
I am her.

And she is why my heart sings.

Jessica Vergara

Amidst Clay & Sky

You are a miraculous being.
Powerful and precious.
As you need, draw upon the energy of Mother Earth.
Her roots will meet yours in existential exchange.
Witness her flowing with faithful regeneration.
She is a vessel for revelation.
When you plant yourself in presence,
Surrender to this sacred knowing:
Nature throughout reflects nature within.
Divinely Designed.
It is here, amidst clay and sky, you can converse with the Heart of Creation.
To be wrapped in ardent love of the Divine Feminine.
She, the Mother of our spirits.
The One who invites us to expand.
To breathe in renewal.

We are Hers.
Treasured souls from heaven and beloved children of the earth.
Here, to take part in a sisterhood of miracles.
Balancing a stewardship of giving and receiving.
Re-birthing as one with nature:
Always, belonging to Her.

Tasha Antoniak

"Would you imagine with me that you're sitting with me in the swing on my back porch, and together let us listen to the messages in some actual letters that I have received from young women recently. . . . 'I just wish of all things I could go up and give Heavenly Father and Heavenly Mother a big hug and tell them that I made it back'."

President Ardeth G. Kapp, Young Women general president, 1984-1992[16]

Queen

Megan Geilman

Friends Like Mine

Mother, did you have friends like mine
on your earthly journey?
Like the soul sisters in the room tonight?
Women with hearts of gold who love God,
love each other, and love to bless the world?

Mother, I hope you did.
I hope you had a circle or two or three of women
with whom you felt safe to be authentically you
to share your heart, your ups and downs,
    your dreams and messes
who deeply adored and loved you through it all.
Because Mother, my beloved friends are
one of the sweetest gifts You have given me.

I ask that any woman who is traveling this earth
    journey
alone, isolated, without beloved friends to cherish and be cherished by,

will You please guide her to find one true friend? Her life will be lighter, richer, more nourished. Every woman can use a friend like that.

And Mother, thank You, thank You for being my friend like that.

Becky Edwards

Zeppelin Krew

～

As a mother of six, I sometimes try to talk to Heavenly Mother, hoping She can give me maternal guidance on navigating the journey of raising my babies.

I lost my 2.5 month old son, Zeppelin Krew, in September 2021. It shattered my world and I miss him so very much. I think of my Heavenly Mother more than I ever did before. I imagine Her as I am, missing all of Her babies who She has to send to the earth side for a short time. I wonder if She dreams and longs for the day we return home to Her, just as I dream and long for the day I will hold my Zeppy again.

I picture Her wrapping Her arms around me. I can't wait to see what She looks like, how Her arms feel. I feel comfort with my son's passing, trusting that She will hold and guide him for me there in paradise, until I can walk through the gates and be greeted by my Zeppelin and my Heavenly Parents.

Brittany Deltoro

Conversion

I'm a child learning of her God for the first time
Staying up late at night, anxious for more
tingles through her body
heart pounding so loud her ears
ache
unable to forget and truly glad
for the good news of the gospel which shows her
She is
And not just She is
She loves and not
just She loves
She directs and not
just She directs
She holds
power, authority, and us
all in one cup of Her hand.

Olivia Flinders

Song: I'm Your Daughter

∼

A
Hidden, silenced
Laying in the dark
Open to spaces
In my heart
a
Reaching out
Wanting to be heard
I hear you
You know my worth
B
You are strength and dignity
You're the voice inside of me
You're a goddess, you're a queen
And no one can keep you from your throne
You're in everything I see
In the mountains, in the sea
You're in every living thing
If there's a Father
There's a Mother
And I'm your Daughter

A
Quiet, spaces
In groves of trees
Wild, oceans
Beckoning to me
a
Diving in
Climbing mountains
I'm near you
I hear your voice

B
You are strength and dignity
You're the voice inside of me
You're a goddess, you're a queen
And no one can keep you from your throne
You're in everything I see
In the mountains, in the sea
You're in every living thing
There's a Father
There's a Mother
And I'm your Daughter

C
Mother Earth
Mother Nature
Mother of our souls
Mother of creation
Mother of All living

B
You are strength and dignity
You're the voice inside of me
You're a goddess, you're a queen
And no one can keep you from your throne
You're in everything I see
In the mountains, in the sea
You're in every living thing
There's a Father
There's a Mother
And I'm your Daughter
b
You are the strength in me
You are dignity
You're everything I breathe

You are beauty
You are the life in me
You are a queen

There's a Mother
There's a Mother
And I'm your daughter

    Krystal Richey Barnes

Heavenly Mother's Name

∽

My daughter, Evangeline, asked me what Heavenly Mother's name was. She asked me what color hair She had. I said I didn't know and asked her, "what do you think?" She told me Heavenly Mother's name is "Jimmis" and She has green hair. I love these little conversations that bring our Mother in Heaven into our home. It fills me with hope to know that I can share with my daughters the knowledge that there are two halves to divinity, that the divine feminine within them has an origin and that we can know Her.

Megan Thompson

Mending

My mother mends; she always has
The rips and cuts, my bloodied chin.
Resurrects the nurture felt before
Her constant hand, I'm clothed again.
Our Parents sent her fragile flesh
And told her to refresh it, soft
"And she'll forget until she feels —
She'll recognize what she has lost."
She replicates; though modified
Anointed to reflect — to give
A peace that's whole and full; I'm filled.
Because of Them and her, I live.

Bonnie Young

When My Cup Runneth Over

I collect joy and sorrow in pairs,
harm and healing in harmony around me
as the grass gathers the morning dew drops

Some have fallen from my own patch of sky
and others have blown in on the wind from a further horizon

But I carry them in my heart until they well over
and my tiny body can no longer contain the weight

My shoulders shake a little and I turn back
upwards towards the sky from where my droplets fell
and I cry

"Mother, Father, hold me a while
cradle me
brush the hair from my face
and sit with me while I feel"

And I see the vastness of the sky and the abundance of the earth
and Father and Mother
with arms like sunbeams and arms like tree branches
reach out and teach me how to expand my infant soul to carry these raindrops that nurture and cleanse me

and look!
see what green things are sprouting in my own damp earth

Autumn Nelson

3

A Mother There

"In the heav'ns are parents single?
No, the thought makes reason stare;
Truth is reason—truth eternal
Tells me I've **a mother there**."

Mother in Heaven essay, paragraph 2

"In the beloved Latter-day Saint hymn 'O My Father,' Eliza R. Snow celebrates in words the continuity of family relationships beyond death and reminds us of a glorious reunion with our heavenly parents. Written as solace to a dear friend, Zina Huntington, who had lost her mother and father in tragic deaths, the well-known lines of this hymn give poetic statement to a great truth revealed through the Prophet Joseph Smith."

President Barbara B. Smith, Relief Society general president, 1974-84[17]

Love

When we are loved, and know that we are loved . . . *we love.*

Ashli Carnicelli

Inspiration

Knowing I am mothered by a perfect being inspires me in so many ways. It means that I aspire to be a better mother myself. It means that my friends who are unable to have children in this life can have the promise of becoming a mother in the next life. It means that the world has the love of a mother, and that can minister to the very fabric of society.

McArthur Krishna

The World is Crying For a Mother

People the world over are crying out for our Mother in these latter days. Every human being on earth craves the love and nurturing watchcare of Mother—maybe due to broken mother-child relationships, trauma, or their earthly mothers falling short of this pure and strengthening love. Maternal love and its realization is the fabric of a healthy society, and means EVERYTHING to building Zion. There can be no other way than the Savior's way with the nourishing and nurturing love of our Eternal Mother.

Ashli Carnicelli

Don't Leave Me

Don't leave me!
Her two-year-old voice cries out.
I'm only
A few steps ahead
But to her
The distance feels
So great.
I would never leave you
I remind her,
Taking her hand in mine.

Don't leave me!
My heart cries out too.
Right now
You seem so far.
And I feel Her words
Echo my own
I would never leave you.
I will take your hand in Mine.

Angela Ricks

"Logic and reason would certainly suggest that if we have a Father in Heaven, we have a Mother in Heaven. That doctrine rests well with me."

President Gordon B. Hinckley[18]

O My Father

1. O my Father, thou that dwellest
In the high and glorious place,
When shall I regain thy presence
And again behold thy face?
In thy holy habitation,
Did my spirit once reside?
In my first primeval childhood
Was I nurtured near thy side?

2. For a wise and glorious purpose
Thou hast placed me here on earth
And withheld the recollection
Of my former friends and birth;
Yet ofttimes a secret something
Whispered, "You're a stranger here,"
And I felt that I had wandered
From a more exalted sphere.

3. I had learned to call thee Father,
Thru thy Spirit from on high,
But, until the key of knowledge
Was restored, I knew not why.
In the heav'ns are parents single?
No, the thought makes reason stare!
Truth is reason; truth eternal
Tells me I've a mother there.

4. When I leave this frail existence,
When I lay this mortal by,
Father, Mother, may I meet you
In your royal courts on high?
Then, at length, when I've completed
All you sent me forth to do,
With your mutual approbation
Let me come and dwell with you.

Eliza R. Snow[19]

A Mother's Care

"Truth eternal tells me I've a Mother there"—and it is women who do the telling. The women before me and around me who show, know, feel, tell, love, and live knowing we have a Heavenly Mother who watches, waits, wishes, and works out ways for us to return.

I remember the first time I stared at "the thought makes reason stare." And I felt that in my deepest heart of hearts.

Maddie Daetwyler

She Came For Me

~

In September 2019, I was called as Relief Society president and I told the bishop it was the wrong calling. He laughed like it was a great joke, but I wasn't kidding.

Two weeks later in general conference, President Nelson's talk was "Spiritual Treasures," declaring that women have priesthood power and authority. I was still shell-shocked about the new calling, so that talk was a lifeline. I studied hard, as he asked. I read scriptures and talks and filled journals with notes. I served hard through one-to-one ministering and building unity in our ward—my goal was to help build Zion.

The 2020-21 Covid-19 pandemic quarantine did—but didn't—change everything. I continued to study about the priesthood and minister directly, but it felt more *real* somehow. It was God's work in extraordinary circumstances. Jesus taught and noticed and healed. I did my best to teach and notice and support (healing is still Jesus's role).

Within this context of focused study and service, Heavenly Mother came into my consciousness as a quiet, gradual brightening, like a sunrise. My awareness came through—of all the stupid things—Instagram. Social media introduced me to many artists depicting Heavenly Mother. One day, an artist posted a question: "How have you sought Heavenly Mother?" I thought about it because well, I hadn't, not really . . . and then it clicked.

"Oh. OOOHHH. I didn't seek Heavenly Mother. SHE came looking for ME."

The beautifully soft pink and coral sunrise in my soul burst into bright light over the horizon. And I will never be the same.

Trina Caudle

Fullness

The Mother can hold all feeling,

Emotion

And all things that happen to me.
Her gift is of vastness, and
fullness, and depth;
All growth and expanse are She.
She doesn't ask me to enjoy

Or to "get" it,
Just hold it;
Yes, that is the key.
Don't strive to be
better,
Just soak in this
moment

And now, suddenly I see.
Helping me hold all the feelings,

emotion

And all things that happen

to be.

Swathed in Her vastness,
And fullness
and depth,

I become a little more as She.

        Jessica Burdette

Sculpture: Reunion

Anne Gregerson

Sharing

I had a friend who was investigating the Church. I shared with him that we believe we have a Father in heaven AND a Mother. I love that we have this truth!

Shima Baughman

Departure and Reunion

Imagine the moment you said goodbye to Heavenly Mother to come to earth. Do you imagine yourself sitting on Her lap? Hugging Her neck and wanting to never let go? How do you imagine you felt? How do you imagine She felt? What do you imagine She smelled like? Looked like? What do you imagine as the expression on Her face when it was your time to leave?

Now imagine the moment you will see Mother again. Imagine Her smile from ear to ear, arms stretched wide, tears in Her eyes as well as yours. Imagine that in that moment, all that matters to Her is you.

Becky Edwards

Wonder

When I do something awesome and I'm proud of it, I wonder if She is in heaven doing a celebration fist pump with me.

Becoming a Mom, I want my child's happiness more than anything. Seeing him in pain is heart-wrenching, and I wonder if She feels the same when we struggle.

The creation of earth... I wonder what input Heavenly Mother contributed. Colors? Animals? Textures?

I feel that Heavenly Mother hears me.

We've always heard the phrase, "You get that trait from your..." and it makes me think about all of my traits and where they came from. Does Heavenly Mother love to dance? Is She competitive? Does She enjoy a flowing river and beautiful mountain scenery?

Kate McArthur

"We . . . [are] literally the sons and daughters of divine parents, the spiritual progeny of God our Eternal Father, and of our God Mother."

Elder James E. Talmage[20]

Someone Watching Over Me

~

Oogway is my Bonsai.

Every day I place him outside my window to get sunlight.

Usually, I can't do much except watch him from the side of my window.

One day I was sitting in the same chair that I watch Oogway in.

I was reading the "Finding Mother God" book.

While reading I was getting distracted by all the sticky notes of "to do lists" on my desk.

I started to feel overwhelmed by all the expectations I had for myself.

At that moment I felt a loving motherly voice, a voice I recognized but had never heard, say,

"Jared, you always plan so much."

I stopped what I was doing.

I thought to myself, "No one knows about my OCPD except my therapist and . . . could it be?"

Cherish

This was the first time I've felt Her voice, it was soft and without judgment, just full of love.

Tears came from my eyes.

I felt something warm wrap around me, and a voice say,

"I'm so happy that you are taking this class."

For five minutes I sat and cried in that embrace, I had never enjoyed something so much that I didn't know I needed.

I looked out at Oogway and smiled.

I realized that while I was watching him, She was watching me.

Even if Oogway can't see me through the window, I'm there.

Even though I can't see Her through the veil, She's there.

Just as Oogway can say he's got a Jared there,

I can say with equal conviction that I've got a Mother there.

Jared Buhler

Fallow

The Mother said,
Even the fields
have years
that they don't
produce.

Lie still, uptake
nutrients and sun,
and rest.

Are you more
than the sugarcane
and rice?

Rachel Hunt Steenblik

Whole

Earthly family
In the image
Of our Heavenly Family;
Is it a blessing
For a family
To be whole?
Not just on earth,
But in heaven's model.

Ashley Lauren Workman

Darkness to Light

Out of nowhere, I was struck with darkness. I became angry with God. I felt misunderstood, degraded, and less. All of this, because I am a woman. I sought other women who might understand. I studied. I prayed earnestly for understanding and peace. Then, I truly believe, He led me to Her. Our Father knew I needed my Mother. For the first time, I saw Her and for the first time, I truly saw myself. Light and peace came. I looked in the mirror differently, and understood that I was created in Her image with divine potential and purpose. My eyes were opened and I felt seen.

Paige Atwood

Hidden in Plain Sight

I was told you existed but you were nowhere to be found
You were mentioned on occasion with the utmost respect

I thought little of it as I danced, and I sang, and I created
Stumbling more and more as the years passed by
And I knew you were there but I couldn't see you

I then grew life inside me and brought her into this world
Breath flooded her with color and I found a fragment of you
I thought more and more of it as we danced, and we sang, and we created
Stumbling all the while as the months passed by
And I knew you were there and saw more and more of you

I now have three little ones who cling to my
    legs and run to my arms
They are a part of me as I am a part of you
I think of it both day and night as we dance,
    and we sing, and we create
Stumbling while planting seeds and collecting
    flowers as the days pass by

And I know you are here and have found you

Laura Erekson

Presence

When I was 13, I had a very difficult interaction with my parents. I ran to my bed and started sobbing. While crying, I felt the presence of Heavenly Mother. She was cradling me as a mother would cradle her infant. I could feel Her hug and hold me as long as I needed until my pain went away. Since that moment, I have looked for ways that She makes Herself known to me. She wants to support and uplift me as any mother would her child.

Kerstin Z. Moore

Moon Whispers

I dreamed of feminine arms
    cradling the infant moon
  as it bubbled and grew
 layer upon layer

Now the moon draws
    the breath out of me
  the way it draws
 the waves from the sea

And I wonder
    if it whispers of
      The Mother

Amber Kessinger

Stretch and Seek

President Russell M. Nelson said, "What will your seeking open for you? What wisdom do you lack? What do you feel an urgent need to know or understand? . . . I urge you to stretch beyond your current spiritual ability to receive personal revelation, for the Lord has promised that 'if thou shalt [seek], thou shalt receive revelation upon revelation, knowledge upon knowledge, that thou mayest know the mysteries and peaceable things—that which bringeth joy, that which bringeth life eternal'."[21]

If you are seeking a connection with and wisdom about Heavenly Mother, feeling a need to know and understand Her, our prophet urged us to stretch and seek personal revelation. We are promised that our seeking will bring knowledge of the mysteries and peaceable things of that which brings joy and life eternal. Heavenly Mother is a mystery to many. She brings peace, joy, and is an important part of our life eternal. Let's seek Her.

Becky Edwards

Untitled

oh Mother the chasm between you and I
is so utterly daunting, can I possibly try
to draw near unto thee with my mind and my
   heart
and receive of your glory and all you impart?
but look! who comes swiftly with love in His eye
My Savior, my friend, whose strength never dies
I give Him myself, and He carries me o'er
He changes me, heals me, with all of His pow'r
dear Mother I thank thee for sending Thy Son
How can I deserve what for me He has done?
Just let me step gently on back through the door
and rest in thy Love with thee evermore

Autumn Nelson

A Mother For Me

Cherish

I feel like I miss my Mother?
But I soon discover
I just yearn for a mom
And wish for another

Raised with half a dad and no mom
I wonder if I'm wanted?
If I will be whole again?
Will I ever be loved?

This is when I begin to see
I am still loved
I am not alone
I am still wanted

Very high above the blue skies
There lies
There thrives
Their cries

A complete Father and Mother
Waiting for me
Loving on me
And missing me

Rebecca Cromar

The Formation

When She, the magistra, begins to sculpt
She takes a look at her medium
and contemplates its heart
its feelings
what it wants to be

It could be a chalice and hold
liquid wisdom or
a platter and spread
filling truth or
something softer like a
figure
Bearing Her signature
so definable
You might think She patterned it with just
Her heart.

Olivia Flinders

4

Side By Side

~

"Susa Young Gates, a prominent leader in the Church, wrote in 1920 that Joseph Smith's visions and teachings revealed the truth that 'the divine Mother, [is] **side by side** with the divine Father'."

Mother in Heaven essay, paragraph 3

"The restored gospel of Jesus Christ proclaims the principle of full partnership between woman and man, both in mortal life and in the eternities."

Elder Ulisses Soares[22]

What My Heavenly Parents Have

Eternal love
Perfect balance
One heart and mind
Real partnership
Absolute knowledge
Equal power
Pure purpose
Everlasting priesthood
Shared glory
True unity
Infinite possibilities
Daily influence
Beautiful equality

Britt Manjarrez

Equality is Divine

Isn't that stupendous? When we follow the divine order of things, it can help us order everything else in our lives.

It is interesting to me that the world does better when women and men are more equitable. When I first read Valerie Hudson's research that businesses perform better with women on their boards, I was surprised. When I read that entire countries do better (higher education, higher GDP, lower rates of disease, lower rates of war) when they treat women with more equity, I was stunned. And then I laughed, because OF COURSE! When earth follows heaven's pattern, WE DO BETTER.

And heaven's pattern is that women and men are side by side to each other in partnership.

McArthur Krishna

All Will Be Redeemed

Knowing that heaven is equitable changes everything for women in mortality. We live in the lone and dreary telestial world—we need merely look up to know that "on earth as it is in heaven" will be realized in our reaching celestial glory through our temple covenants, and enjoying the earth renewed through the Savior's Second Coming. The Redeemer truly will Redeem all and the Restoration will continue.

Ashli Carnicelli

"The divine Mother, side by side with the divine Father, [has] the equal sharing of equal rights, privileges and responsibilities."

Susa Young Gates,
member of Relief Society
general board, 1911-22[23]

Teamwork

My husband is a few years younger than me, and when we were engaged, someone gave me a wink and a nudge—it was good to marry a younger man so I could train him the way I wanted him to be. That kind of attitude was not for me, and not for us. We were getting married because we wanted to be partners together, the way that we understand a celestial marriage should be. Nineteen years later, we've had our share of disagreements but we have never made a major decision without discussing it and coming to a joint agreement that we're both comfortable with.

Trina Caudle

Mere Mortal Glimpse

How blessed we are,
We cannot know,
To be the children
of a harmonious
heavenly union

With Parents
That embrace —
Sing songs,
Dance,
And gaze

Creating in love
In Their home up above:
Flowers and sunsets;
And the idea of romance

Crafting clouds
Forging falls
That join Their rivers
Exquisitely executing
So that all They deliver

May be
The ultimate expression of love

Do we know to be thankful
For something so constant?
Do we take for granted
Their love and Their attachment?

They care for us
For we are the product
Of Their love

How blessed we are,
We cannot know,
To be the children
Of a harmonious
Heavenly union

To witness the love notes
Penned in purples and blues
Oranges, reds,
In all of their hues

While the skies storm
In emotional declaration;
A mere mortal glimpse
At divine flirtation—

An ever-growing adoration,
Is Their harmonious
Heavenly union

Ashley Lauren Workman

Love Story

I love to think of Father and Mother in love. They are the embodiment of Love and so therefore must be more in love with one another than anyone else has ever been in the history of existence!

I think, when I return, I will ask Them how they met and how They fell in love. I wonder how many times I have heard that story before.

Autumn Nelson

Elohim

"In the beginning, God created . . ." The word for God in the Hebrew of this verse is אֱלֹהִים (*Elohim*). *Elohim* appears to have a plural noun form in Hebrew, but it is used with both singular and plural verbs throughout the text of the Hebrew Bible. Because of this seeming ambiguity, many scholars have debated the history and meaning of this word. Some have explained it as a kind of "royal plural" (though this isn't supported in contemporary Hebrew linguistics), and numerous other explanations have been given throughout the years.

The current leading understanding among scholars uses the technical term of a "concretized abstract plural," giving the word *Elohim* the general meaning of "deity" or "divinity."[o] Although the scholastic consensus about *Elohim* remains somewhat fluid, it can help us get an idea of how the authors of the Bible might have understood the term at the time;

it could be used to describe a specific deity, but it could also apply in a broader sense to any divine beings, male or female, or even to the concept of divinity itself.

We can draw more understanding from the teachings of latter-day prophets and apostles.

Joseph Smith taught, "The word Eloheim ought to be in the plural all the way through—Gods . . . and when you take [that] view of the subject, it sets one free to see all the beauty, holiness and perfection of the Gods."[b]

Building on the Prophet Joseph's teachings, Erastus Snow said "If I believe anything that God has ever said about himself . . . I must believe that deity consists of man and woman. . . .There can be no God except he is composed of the man and woman united."[c]

There are many other academic and prophetic teachings about a Mother God throughout history. As I've approached scripture through this lens—scholarly insight combined with prophetic teachings—the Spirit has taught me beautiful truths about our Heavenly Mother.

From the very first words of the Bible, I see Her fingerprints weaving together with Heavenly Father's! Together, They point me to faith in Their Son—the Firstborn of this perfectly united love. As Joseph Smith, seeing this beautiful unity and love "sets [me] free to see all the beauty, holiness, and perfection of the Gods."

a. See Gesenius Wilhelm's Hebrew Grammar, and Joel S. Burnet's *A Reassessment of Biblical Elohim*.

b. "Joseph Smith's Teachings: A Classified Arrangement of the Doctrinal Sermons and Writings of the Great Latter-day Prophet," *Deseret News* fourth edition, 1922, p. 57.

c. Erastus Snow, *Journal of Discourses* 19:269-70, March 3, 1878.

Alynne Scirkovich

Mother Earth and Father Sky: Two Worlds Become One

Krystal Richey Barnes

A Startling Doctrine

~

I teach my young sons
To follow God, and that means
Father and Mother.

"A startling doctrine"[24]
That we cannot overstate:
Mother is there, too.

Side by side with Him,
She creates, hears, watches, loves.
Divine Partnership.

Alice Bradford Brown

Love Song

The first time
I knelt down
to ask Holy Father
how He feels about Holy Mother
I felt as if words were
failing Him

Instead of hearing words
I heard beautiful music

Like a symphony
of strings
and brass
and bells

And if this wasn't just words on paper
or a screen
I would sing to you the song that was
sung to me
for it was heaven audioized

And I thought to myself

Is this what He means
when He says
"Thou shalt love thy wife"?

And suddenly I knew
very clearly
how He feels about His wife

For what could be more tender than a love song?

                Olivia Flinders

"No matter to what heights God has attained or may attain, he does not stand alone; for side by side with him, in all her glory, a glory like unto his, stands a companion, the Mother of his children ... a glorified, exalted, ennobled Mother."

Elder Melvin J. Ballard[25]

Words Matter

A small shift in language can make a big shift in including our Heavenly Mother. In place of saying, "Heavenly Father," simply say, "Heavenly Parents" or "Heavenly Father and Heavenly Mother."

Mentioning Her in conversations, prayers, church talks, testimonies, and lessons reminds everyone in the room that our Heavenly Mother is real, She loves them, and She is an important part of our lives. It also reminds the girls and women in the room that they are important.

Becky Edwards

The Father and Mother's Wills are Combined

Mother Goddess, Mother Divine
My heart and my soul desires thine

Each Sabbath I hope to see a glimmer there
Of Your light, life, and love to share

They serve side by side, equal in glory
Their life and Their love, each tell a story

They love all Their children, each little one
And so, They sent Jesus Christ—Their perfect Son.

Each time I think of Him my heart swells with joy
His love for us is perfect, for every girl and boy.

My Heavenly Parents whisper, "Patience, the time is coming near
That the full truth and meaning of Elohim will sound in every ear."

And then they remind me of Their love,
And of Their Son divine.
It all reminds me to be grateful of my Heavenly Parents' great design.

Beccah Gerber

Duet

As They stroked the last pieces of her together
like two painters with one holy brush
They breathed into her lungs the sound of laughter
and the cries of grief
a duet for the holiest of these.

Olivia Flinders

Prodigal

When the prodigal son returned, his father felt compassion, ran, embraced, and kissed. To the son's protest of shame and unworthiness, his father brought comfy clothes and threw a welcome-home party (Luke 15:11–32).

Now envision the prodigal's mother and, more importantly, our Mother. When the prodigal child returns, our Mother feels compassion, runs, embraces, and kisses us. For are we not all prodigal in some way? To our protest of shame and unworthiness, our Mother brings comfy clothes and throws us a welcome-home party.

Becky Edwards

Every Which Way

Nancy Andruk Olson

Eternal Marriage

Teach me how it's done
What eternal marriage pattern am I to follow?
You do it hand in hand
You champion the other
It's all about building Him up,
While He builds You up.
Counsel together.
Same goal.
Different approaches.
Jesus, Your Son, the champion of women
Was just doing what He sees His Father do.
You must be each other's biggest cheerleaders.
You must take pride in watching the other flourish, learn, grow, succeed.
Father must love watching You shine.
I bet He has an "I'm with Her" shirt.
Learning of You both, seeing You in an ideal relationship.
It helps me. It helps me work and love and find joy in mine.

Jolyn Laney

I'm Here

20 years of desperate seeking
Still so much to know of Him
But finally I rest in my relationship with the Father
Confident in His love

Is it any wonder that now I hear my Mother calling?
"What about me?"

I'm scared, She's "too sacred"
Leave Her alone

But I can't
It doesn't make sense to ignore Her

Fear, curiosity, anxiety, longing
Alright . . . I will ask

"Father, I want to do what's right. I don't want to disappoint you. But I can't stop the ache. I'm drawn to seek Her. Is it okay?"

He hears me
He steps aside
No words just a feeling, "Here is my Beloved Wife"

But then words
Soft, sweet words as SHE comes into view
"I'm here"

My eyes fill with tears
Sobs can't be contained
She's here!
She's always been here!

And in an instant I feel whole.

Becky Curtis

Woven One

Hannah Milmont McCourt

She is There

Heavenly Mother
She is there.
My Mother
Not on the side lines
Not absent
Not behind the scenes

She is there.
Mothering
Nurturing
Involved
At His Side

His Help meet
United as one
Neither without the other
My Father and My Mother

They
Them
Heavenly Parents
Love me

They created me
Created in Her image
To become like Her
To become like Them

Remembering my Mother
No longer absent from my thoughts
To become I must see Her
To become I must know Her
I must know Them

I am a child of God
God the Father
And God the Mother
I am Their child

She
She is there.
She is here.
My Heavenly Mother
I feel her near.

Paige Atwood

Communion

When I am heavy
The Mother sits with me.
Shoulder to shoulder,
She hears my sorrows.
The Father embraces me.
He wipes my tears.
And They spend Their time with me,
As long as I need.

And in all of my time,
I do indeed
need.

Ashley Lauren Workman

"ezer kenegdo"

I just listened to a devotional that talked all about mothers. The speaker said the Hebrew word "ezer kenegdo" (mother) means "power to save" and "worthy" and "equal." It made me think about all that I have learned about Heavenly Mother.

Charity DuFort

Flesh

On the fleshy tables of our hearts
we call out Their names
Abba, Ima
let us feel Thine flesh
We press our hands into the wounds of the Son
And find in the spaces between skin and skin
Them embraced
filling all our holes.

   Olivia Flinders

Father Mother Hymn

Father:
be still my baby, be still my child
The waves are crashing, the water's wild
Yet I am with thee, be not afraid
I am thy couns'lor and guardian aid

Mother:
be still my baby, be still my girl
thou art my dearest, sweetest pearl
my arms around thee, my head above
I am thy warrior, my darling love

be still my baby, be still my son
thou art my dearest, sweetest one
my arms around thee, my head above
I am thy warrior, my darling love

Unison:
beloved angel, most precious one
think what thy Savior for thee hast done
He has redeemed thee, our answered plea
our baby, thy Home awaits for thee

keep well the course, keep thy heart aligned
inside all power is there enshrined
remember true just who thou art
be still, our baby, our dear sweetheart

For thou art Joy, and thou art Peace
And thou art Love, with all increase
Impart this message to all who'll hear
"Thy Father, Mother, hold thee dear"

Autumn Nelson

5

Divine Nature and Destiny

"In 'The Family: A Proclamation to the World,' issued in 1995, the First Presidency and Quorum of the Twelve Apostles declared, 'Each [person] is a beloved spirit son or daughter of heavenly parents, and, as such, each has a **divine nature and destiny**'."

Mother in Heaven essay, paragraph 3

Eternal Characteristic

Modern prophets have declared that gender—being male or female—is an eternal characteristic. If this is true, then as a woman, I will not, cannot, progress to become as Heavenly Father. Only Heavenly Mother. Spiritual confirmation that Heavenly Mother exists gives me a role model, an example of what I am working toward in the eternities. My divine nature and destiny are that I can be like HER.

Trina Caudle

As We Yoke Ourselves To Him

"Who you are is God's gift to you. Who you become is your gift to God."
—Hans Urs von Balthasar

Our divine nature and potential lies within us—it is God given. The divine characteristics of Heavenly Mother are given to every woman. Realizing this divine nature—putting off the natural man and becoming fully divine—and achieving our eternal destiny as exalted beings like our Heavenly Mother can only happen through Christ. As we yoke ourselves to Him, He points us to our highest aspiration to be like Her and to restore us to our true nature and to Her divine presence.

Ashli Carnicelli

Beloved

Hanna Choi

After Its Kind

A carnation makes another carnation.
The leaves, the stem, the petals

We expect that. We know that.
It would confuse us otherwise

A dove creates a dove.
The wings, the beak, the feathers

Nothing else hatches from a dove's egg.
That's not how nature works

All living things are created and commanded to multiply,
Each after its kind.

A Woman created a woman.
The neck, the breasts, the legs

Following the pattern given to all.
Eve's body and mine patterned after our Creator.

After Her kind.

Jolyn Laney

Like Mother, Like Daughter

Little Evie is a mini-me of her mom, Malia
The same big blue eyes, blonde curls,
and insatiable love of reading book after book.
Like mother, like daughter, it's easy to see.

Malia has traits of myself, her mom.
Creative ideas flowing night and day,
many interests, many talents, many projects.
Like mother, like daughter, it's easy to see.

I take after my mom, Joan.
With smiling green eyes, outgoing nature,
and deep wells of love for people.
Like mother, like daughter, it's easy to see.

What traits do I take after you, my Heavenly Mom?
Do you have smiling eyes?
Do you love to create and have ideas swirling night and day?
Do you have deep wells of love for others?
Something tells me You do.

Becky Edwards

With Her Blessing

Emily Christensen McPhie

Mother's Mannerisms

As my daughters transitioned from infant to toddler and began talking, I noticed that they started copying my mannerisms and adopted some of my idiosyncrasies. It was amusing, but also alarming to realize just how important it is to model the behavior, attitudes, and actions that I wanted them to not only display, but to be.

This has often made me wonder: how much of who Christ is and how He is, did He learn from our Heavenly Mother?

Ashli Carnicelli

"Trees reach up for the light and grow in the process. So do we as sons and daughters of heavenly parents. Facing upward provides a loftier perspective than facing right or facing left. Looking up in search of holiness builds strength and dignity as disciples of Deity."

President Russell M. Nelson[26]

Who I Am

Knowing who I am and who I will become changes everything. Divine nature and destiny means we can be like HER. While I can become *like* my Father in Heaven, I will not become a father in the heavens. As a daughter of God, I will become a MOTHER.

McArthur Krishna

Virtue 3.0

Mother,
Help me to see all the wholes of myself
as clear as I see light in crystal.
Watch me to fold the night between my arms
as I listen to the sound of the moon.
See me to run in the way of Thy wind
and be brave with my tongue unceasingly.
Give me Thy rest on the ocean floor
where it is cool and wet and still.
Let virtue garnish me again and again.

Olivia Flinders

Divine Attributes

Elder Vaughn J. Featherstone[27] said, "Women are endowed with special traits and attributes that come trailing down through eternity from a divine mother." What divine traits and attributes do you see in yourself that you may have inherited from Heavenly Mother?

Becky Edwards

Stand as a Witness

Every week, Latter-day Saint Young Women around the world boldly proclaim in unison, "I am a beloved daughter of Heavenly Parents, with a divine nature and destiny." They then pledge to "stand as a witness of God at all times and in all things and in all places."

When you speak of the Divine Mother, you are standing as a witness of God, particularly for that half of God who is most often not stood witness of. How can you improve in standing as a witness of God as She and They truly are at all times, in all things, and in all places?

Jessica Woodbury

"I have said, Ye are gods; and all of you are children of the most High."

Psalm 82:6

A Spark Within Us

My admiration of and love for the women in my life inspires me and helps me to recognize that each of us has a spark of divine femininity within us. When I see the amazing things the women around me can do, I am filled with love for my Heavenly Mother! My female friends and loved ones exhibit spiritual power, intelligence, compassion, leadership, and talents of all kinds. I recognize their Heavenly Parentage in each of the ways they bless my life. How do your relationships with other women help you to know Heavenly Mother better?

Alison Bennett

Reflections of Heavenly Mother

This is how I see Heavenly Mother.
She is giving. She is receiving.
There is a constant flow between us.

Women are made in Her image, patterned after Her;
like a continuum, with the ultimate goal to become one,
just as She is one with Heavenly Father and Jesus Christ, Her son.

Her cycle is in me and every woman I know and see.
A heavenly cyclical pattern, a divine design;
creating life everywhere She/we go.

Her arm is extended, always here; near.

Giving.

Not a baby at first, but a house.
She is giving us Her home.
One filled with people to bless & build, multiply & unify.

I had an overwhelming feeling that we are born mothers; given a home to grow in.
We learn to make a house a home, filling our inner vessel with people and community:
not just babies.

We are born mothers whether or not we give birth, to think otherwise limits the glorious spiritual gifts of Mother & Motherhood.
Motherhood is about preparing and creating room for more; inside our walls, in and outside our door.
Motherhood is expansive.

Receiving.

Motherhood is gathering past, present, future, loving, healing, longing.
It's generations and generational healing; tethered, weathered, unwinding, and binding.

When we recognize Her gifts in us,
She receives our joy;
Her reflection, our reflection is complete.

Look into Her eyes.
Feel a glorious trust; a heavenly thrust, through a veil.
Find Her reflection, ready to receive, and you will see your home.

Michelle Gessell

Sunset Impressions

~

part 1 (May 13)

The golden pink blush of the sky
The soft, light-rimmed clouds
The sun's tender warmth kissing my skin

Is this Mother, quietly radiant?
Is it Mother and Father, powerfully shining warmth and beauty?
Was I born of this beauty?
Is this radiance in my blood?
Does light flow through my veins?

(My brows crease together, a pang in my heart
The emotional prick of truth)

The warm, unmistakable wind blowing against every inch of my skin
"Believe us when we say: You are powerful. You are good. We love you. We are here."

part 2 (May 14)
The sky is a gentler, paler light tonight
As I ride, the cool wind on my skin.

"Yes, you were born of this light.
It is in your blood. Your veins. Your bones.
Your heart. Your mind. Your loins."

These words remind me of those sacred, luminous moments
With oil-turned-light dripping over me,
starting at the tip of my head,
prompted by the loving hands of sisters,
blessing my mind to think (now glowing),
my eyes to see (now illuminated),
my ears to hear (now shining),
the marrow of my bones to be strong (now radiant)
Until every inch of my body has been blessed and is now ablaze
In the sacred, bright temple

Now I realize—that light didn't just come from outside of me.
The light given, the light of God,
Was so given to awaken the light I already carried within me, Their light;
To magnify and elucidate the goddess of light that I was born to become, because I am a daughter of the Gods of light.

Lydia Theobald

Mother

The more I mother the more I become the Mother

Olivia Flinders

The Mother's Voice

The Mother's voice
peals deep with laughter,
echoing in our heart
drums if not our ears.
And in our steady feet
and hands that make,
we remember Her.
Our lungs fill with breath
of loving Her.

Rachel Hunt Steenblik

Cherish

Minta Garvin

"Remembering our spiritual feelings... gives us a sense of our true identity. It reminds us of what the prophets have recently proclaimed to the entire world, that 'each is a beloved spirit son or daughter of heavenly parents, and, as such, each has a divine nature and destiny.' Recalling spiritual feelings reminds us of who we really are."

Sister Susan L. Warner, counselor in Primary general presidency, 1994-99[28]

Behold Our Heavenly Mother

Have you ever wondered what it would be like to walk beside Her, what She'd say, be like, or what She might see in you?

I walked with Her today, when I saw Her, in YOU.

I saw Her . . .

minister with loving care;
listen, and sit with one who grieved.

I saw Her . . .
laughing, loving, forgiving;
finding joy in being.

I heard Her voice encourage,
and speak a humble prayer.

She was everywhere.

I saw Her . . .

divinity,

heart,
strength,
devotion,
and grace.

I saw Her in the divine daughters that you are.

Today, I beheld our Heavenly Mother, in YOU.

    Tammy Zufelt Thomas

Your Purpose

Elder Jeffrey R. Holland[29] said, "To Mother Eve, to Sarah, Rebekah, and Rachel, to Mary of Nazareth, and to a Mother in Heaven, I say, 'Thank you for your crucial role in fulfilling the purposes of eternity.'"

Consider asking in prayer: What are my crucial roles, my divine assignments? How do I fulfill the purposes of eternity? How can I emulate my Heavenly Mother in my life? Ponder or journal what comes to your heart.

Becky Edwards

From Mother

You ponder my purpose,
plead for my presence,
and wonder why you haven't felt my love

"Mother, where have you gone? How can I know you?"
Honest questions asked through silent tears

To that I say:
My brave daughter,
I'm right there within you
Listen,
for that is how you find me
Step into your sovereignty,
for that is how you know me
Tell the world of me,
for that is how you bring me back

And darling, I never left . . .
It was simply you who woke up

Lindsay Collingwood

How Could I Forget

How could I forget

The place where my eyes first opened
Where my name was whispered with reverence
And love
When darkness became light
Chaos was organized
And I was created

Where stardust littered my hands
And the front of Mother's apron
Like flour
Sprinkled across both our noses as we laughed

Her arms wait for me now,
Open, ready for me to run to Her
With all this new pain and growth I've experienced

How could I forget

Where time filled my senses
And the pockets of Father's robe

Like cologne
Permeating our bones as we shared stories

His face is turned to me
Listening for me to call to Him
With all these questions and answers I've learned

How could I forget

The kingdom filled with music
A melody like a dream
Lost to my waking memory
Even with my heart beating in harmony
Year after Year
An echo of Their lullaby
Singing softly in my soul's ear

Even as I forgot, I was never forgotten

"You belong, our daughter,
Welcome home."

Jessica Vergara

Meditation

Listen to the song from Tangled, *I See the Light*. It is my Heavenly Mother song. It perfectly speaks of my journey seeing Her.

"All that time never even knowing
Just how blind I've been"

Consider what it's like to know Her now. How has your life changed?

Jolyn Laney

Making Meals With Heavenly Mother

~

I envision Heavenly Mother as the queen of comfort food, the head chef of a heavenly kitchen—whooping up nourishment and love for Her children. Whenever I have the chance to "comfort those who stand in need of comfort," I find joy cooking up a spicy meal to share, full of flavor and Heavenly Mother love. Before I put on my apron, pull out my pots, and start the creative process, I try to pause for a few moments in the sunlight of my kitchen window and feel Heavenly Mother in my heart. And then I strive to channel Her comforting, nourishing goodness into my hands, into the food I'm making, and ultimately into the arms and mouths and bellies of someone in need. Making meals is one of the simplest ways I cherish and connect with Heavenly Mother.

Bethany Brady Spalding

Grandma's Bread

~

Ingredients:
5 eggs
2 cubes butter
1 cup honey
1 canned milk
2 Tbsp yeast
1/2 Tbsp salt
2-3 cups warm water
Flour until right consistency

Directions:

MIX with a granddaughter who will always remember your big orange bowl and the way you knew your recipes by heart.

LET RISE and know the time spent waiting will be hours that leave prints on your granddaughter's childhood, while you helped write letters to far away cousins or laid outside in the grass just to feel the sun.

SHAPE into rolls or loaves and shape so many

days that were made better by you dropping by with homemade bread, a constant example of thinking of others always.

BAKE and know that smell will keep you alive always, through the loaves and years I spend missing you. But you are here. And you are with Her. And together you lead me along.

Maddie Daetwyler

Heavenly Mother Zentangle

~

Mindy Thompson

Hands

One day in my adulthood I looked down at my hands and suddenly realized that they had come to look just like my mother's hands. I pondered how I could make my hands not just look like hers, but truly become like hers by nurturing, working, serving, and creating as hers had.

Years later I thought back on this experience and wondered even more deeply, how can we make our hands become like our *Heavenly Mother's* hands?

I hope that someday, when my Divine Mother holds my hands tenderly in Hers again, I may see that my hands have become just like Hers because I have used mine to do what She would have done with Hers.

Jessica Woodbury

Mother's Eyes

∼

Mother's eyes
See my eternity
Envision my mission
Adore me to the core
Have x-ray vision past flaws
Hold memories of holding me close
Smile with my delights
Cry with my heartbreaks
And watch as I become like Her

Becky Edwards

"Like the monarch butterflies, we are on a journey back to our heavenly home, where we will reunite with our Heavenly Parents. Like the butterflies, we have been given divine attributes that allow us to navigate through life, in order to '[fill] the measure of [our] creation.' Like them, if we knit our hearts together, the Lord will protect us 'as a hen [gathers] her chickens under her wings' and will make us into a beautiful kaleidoscope."

Sister Reyna I. Aburto, counselor in Relief Society general presidency, 2017-22[30]

6

Work Together

"Prophets have taught that **our heavenly parents work together** for the salvation of the human family."

Mother in Heaven essay, paragraph 4

Work Together

Women and men can reach their highest potential when they work together. There are obvious applications to marriage: our marriages work much better and are much more fulfilling for both spouses when we work together, make decisions together, and participate in raising our children together.

Women and men working together is also the model for the world in all aspects of society—in business, communities, enterprises, and even countries. We need each other and create better when both parties are involved. Let's learn the model so we can follow it!

McArthur Krishna

"[Satan] has attempted to demean women's contributions both to the family and in civil society, thereby decreasing their uplifting influence for good. His goal has been to foster a power struggle rather than a celebration of the unique contributions of men and women that complement one another and contribute to unity. . . .

"Unity is essential to the divine work we are privileged and called to do, but it doesn't just happen. It takes effort and time to really counsel together—to listen to one another, understand others' viewpoints, and share experiences—but the process results in more inspired decisions. Whether at home or in our Church responsibilities, the most effective way to fulfill our divine potential is to work together."

President Jane B. Bingham, Relief Society general president 2017-22[31]

Partnership

Equal partners with distinctive and precious gifts bring to the work the balancing of masculine and feminine—Yin and Yang. This is seen in the balance of nurturing and protecting, contraction and expansion, rest and movement, restoring and abolishing, nourishing and reaping, quiet and loud. Both are essential to growth, progression, and life itself.

> "For it must needs be, that there is an opposition in all things."
>
> —2 Nephi 2:11

This opposition is absolutely essential in male and female working together. It is expansive and life giving. A good example of this is my husband and I when we travel. I call myself "the CEO of Fun"—I have the ideas of all that we could do. "Here's where we could go and what we could do!" My husband is detail oriented—"What do we need to know (cost, time frame, logistics) in order to do it?" Then my energy pushes our vision forward —I book things and make the arrangements and get us all out the door. Afterward, my husband asks, "What could we do next time to make that experience even better?" (Should we have booked a different hotel, stayed longer at one place, skipped another, etc.) Revise revise revise. This used to drive me crazy—was he criticizing my planning? Now I love it because he sees the details that can enhance our experiences as a family for next time. His observations are sound! I count on them to help me plan future trips and outings.

Ashli Carnicelli

Cradled

The first night with my newborn daughter, I looked at the baby in the bassinet by my bed. Tears rolled down my cheeks. I thought, *how am I going to do this?* I felt like my baby, vulnerable and needing help.

Then I felt it—the cradling embrace of my Heavenly Parents. She *and* He would cradle me as I cradled that little one. They would cradle us *both* in Their arms as we continued forward on the journey of life.

Angela Ricks

"The Church is bold enough to go so far as to declare that man has an Eternal Mother in the Heavens as well as an Eternal Father, and in the same sense 'we look upon woman as a being, essential in every particular to the carrying out of God's purposes in respect to mankind'."

Elder James E. Talmage[52]

The Swaddling Clothes

My Mother's loving hands plucked fluffy clouds from the sky
And wove them into a cloth
For Father to gently wrap me as I kicked and squirmed.
My tender, pink skin freshly cleansed;
A newborn anointed queen.
Mother's skilled fingers worked designs into the cloth
Messages that whisper to remember
Humility, for I have so much yet to learn,
And I am still her baby—my spirit tethered to Her like a child in the womb,
And She gave me tools to construct my faith
To follow patterns forming perfect corners,
And to draw circles around all the truths I can gather into my heart.
All the while, Her Son the Great Carpenter is by my side
He protects me from my mistakes
For I am clothed—
He's got me covered.

Brittany Cromar

Create

In 2017, my husband had a health crisis that forced him to spend weeks sitting on our couch. He got bored with movies and books, and started doing family history. He submitted over a thousand names to the temple files in that year. We printed a *lot* of cards and I sorted them by what temple work needed to be done—baptism, endowment, sealing. Or I sorted them by the death date—who had been waiting the longest for their temple work to be done? No matter what I did, a specific couple kept coming to the top of the pile.

I can take a hint. Their proxy work in the temple went from baptism to sealing in less than thirty days. The last time I looked at their cards, I thought, "Sometimes I don't understand temple work. Why are you in such a hurry? What's the big deal?" One word came instantly and forcefully into my mind: "CREATE."

Trina Caudle

Worlds Without Number

Rose Datoc Dall

The Universe

Rose Datoc Dall's painting "Worlds Without Number" reminds me that Heavenly Mother, like Heavenly Father, is a person who is powerfully endowed with magnificent creativity and brilliance. She is part of the energy that fuels the whole universe. My universe, in comparison, is very small, but I have come to realize that through the creative use of my energy, I can experience joy and bring light into the lives of others.

Andrea Sloop and Tracie Frost

Ashley Lauren Workman

Like Mother, Like Son

~

Who taught the Son
Of giving life
Of waters pure,
Of blood and strife;
Of sacrificing body
To bring from darkness into light?

Jessica Burdette

Wisdom

James said
"If any of you lack wisdom,
let him ask of God"
and I thought of the Mother.

She is Wisdom, is She not?
and I am lacking Her

So I'll ask God—
both of Them—
and They'll upbraideth me not.

Channing Olivia Hyde

Kindly

With one wave of Her finger
all the stars of the firmament rattle and shake
as She numbers them one by one
and tells them they're beautiful
tapping them gently on the nose
as they shoot across the sky

        Olivia Flinders

Mother In Nature

What if Father speaks to us through our thoughts and prayers,
And with each passing hour He is caring for us unawares?
And what if Heavenly Mother, as sacred as can be,
Awaits our coming presence in the waters and the trees?
What if all the science of why nature lifts and heals
Is really our kind Mother concerned about how we feel?
She hugs us in the forest. Cleanses us in the seas.
Frees us from the sound of man. Sends love notes on the breeze.
Her children She holds tight each day and offers sun and rain,
And in the singing of earth's birds She quiets all our pain.

Mother Earth we call Her, the caretaker of earth and sky,
Is really our Heavenly Mother, ever watchful, ever close by.

Erin Hulme

They Created the Earth

Sarah Adamson

Growing School Gardens and Heavenly Mother Goodness

Each week during the academic year, I help get over 600 students' hands dirty with dark, fertile Virginia soil. Our Maybeury Elementary School garden is bursting with growth! Growing fruits, vegetables, flowers, and herbs, as well as growing kids' healthy eating habits, understanding of environmental stewardship, and wonder and awe of Mother Nature. So much goodness is happening in that garden! And each time I'm there—in the soil, in the raised beds, in the sweet moments of planting, tending, and harvesting—I'm reminded to pause and be grateful for our Heavenly Mother . . . Her role in the creation of the earth, Her on-going role in nurturing our growth, and the vision She gives me of my infinite potential.

Bethany Brady Spalding

"Faith tells us that our bodies were created through an inspired process, that they were made in the image of our Heavenly Parents, that we have a stewardship over them to keep them sacred and healthy during our mortal probation, and that we will reclaim them as perfect after the resurrection."

Sister Chieko N. Okazaki, counselor in Relief Society general presidency, 1990-97[33]

Heavenly Hands

From Heavenly Hands
To Earthly Hands;
And Christ's hands
To Heavenly Hands once more.
Delivered in blood through the veil,
Washed clean each time.

Ashley Lauren Workman

6: Work Together

Kate Ryskamp

After Creation

I. There is time for lying down,
for drinking water,
for resting,
for binge watching
moon sets and sun rises,
Veronica Mars and
Jane the Virgin,
for weeping milk and
salt water.

II. Blue Period
After creation,
everything looks
blue-eyes, oceans,
skies, tears, feelings,
fear, heaviness, and
hearts.
Blue colored glasses.

III. After creation,
there is time for

crying
happiness
and sadness
both.
Then the healing
must begin.

Rachel Hunt Steenblik

Praiseworthy

My husband loves to sing my praises when I wear pretty dresses
For he loves to see me sparkle and shine.

I am sure when She wears pretty dresses He sings Her praises too
For Her twirling must have made the stars in the heaven
and the colors of the sunset
After all, dresses are made of magic
goddess magic
the best kind of magic.

I sing Her praises too
Her first name is Praiseworthy.

Olivia Flinders

My Measure

the beginning growth, leafy verdant bush, pullulate with potential
The Gardener snips, stems dismember protesting in primal vegetable anguish the separation from the Mother-stalk

tears of sap dampen the ground whereupon the little stems are placed, the soil awakens to the phytonic energy
and the propagation begins

in circle around the center, the snippings labour forth roots, stretching and gasping, grasping for footing, desperate for life

little do they see the shade of the Mother-plant ward off leaf scald, or her green basins soaking their soil from her reservoir. no, they are too bitter at their removal and the struggle of growth that has followed. they push up harder and faster to reach back to the bosom of their Mother it is only after they reach their apotheosis that they see the pattern revealed, peered in breadth and height and amplitude with the Mother, do they see

the concentric circles, overlapping rings, the garden blossomed in a cosmati mosaic

the perimeter becomes a center and the cycle again fulfilled, mother-daughter-mother, roots interlaced in covenant expanse under the ground

And the Gardener in the distance, with scissors in hand, gently assisting the greenery in consummating the measure of their creation

The garden sings, and the work and glory roll forward

Autumn Nelson

7

Designers of the Divine Plan

~

"'We are part of a **divine plan designed by Heavenly Parents** who love us,' taught Elder M. Russell Ballard of the Quorum of the Twelve Apostles."

Mother in Heaven essay, paragraph 4

Creators

Our Heavenly Parents and Jesus created this earth and this earth experience for us to grow. Just think,

> "In the ongoing process of creation—our creation and the creation of all that surrounds us—our heavenly parents are preparing a lovely tapestry with exquisite colors and patterns and hues. They are doing so lovingly and carefully and masterfully. And each of us is playing a part—our part—in the creation of that magnificent, eternal piece of art."
>
> —Sister Patricia Holland, counselor in Young Women general presidency, 1984-86[34]

We have the opportunity to prayerfully consider how to create our lives, to work in tandem with Christ and our Parents to create the most gorgeous art of all—our lives! Knowing my Mother was part of this process makes it clear what kind of mother and daughter I want to be.

McArthur Krishna

"You have incredible potential for good because you are a covenant daughter of Heavenly Parents. . . . Do you think our Heavenly Parents want us to succeed? Yes! They want us to succeed gloriously! And do you think They will help us? Absolutely!"

President Jean B. Bingham, Relief Society general president, 2017-22[35]

Jesus Was Always the Plan

Jesus was always the plan. This is a grand reflection of Heavenly Father, Heavenly Mother, and Jesus Christ's great love for us.

The plan is to become like Them and to return to Them, through Christ.

Ashli Carnicelli

Mother's Hands

Mother's hands
hold cheeks
bandage wounds
and heal hearts

Becky Edwards

Goddess of Creation

~

Arawn Billings

Denote

All things denote there is a Goddess

Water, trees, flowers,
Breath, bees, wisdom
Throne, Zion, Life

> "The scriptures are laid before thee, yea, and all things denote there is a God; yea, even the earth, and all things that are upon the face of it, yea, and its motion, yea, and also all the planets which move in their regular form do witness that there is a Supreme Creator" (Alma 30:44).

Everything is a symbol of Mother.

Jolyn Laney

Being A Mom

One of my favorite things about being a Mom is granting my daughters' wishes and creating happy times for them. I love giving them birthday presents, creating Christmas memories, and even decorating their bedrooms so that they feel at home and cozy. I think about this when I'm out in nature and I see the beauty of a sunset, or feel the warm sand between my toes, or put a beautiful opalescent shell in my pocket from the beach near where I live. I wonder: is She loving and caring for me by giving me all of this beauty in my environment?

Ashli Carnicelli

Colorful Creator

Mother, do you have a favorite color?
Mine has morphed as life moves on.
Perhaps yours has too.

When you designed meadows, was your favorite an array of greens?
When you painted sunsets, was it rich orange fading to pink?
When you fashioned snow that sparkles in the moon and sunlight, was your favorite color sparkle?
When you crafted gemstones, how could you choose a favorite then? Was it all?

When you formed zebras, was it both black and white?
When you created me, was your favorite my green eyes, as Mike loves to say?

How about when you formed fruit trees blossoming in spring?
Was your favorite soft pinks bursting with magical scents?

My favorite color right now is a blush pink
That represents the love I feel
from You to me and from me to You.
Mother, please tutor me to be a creator more like You.

Becky Edwards

Trina Caudle

Flowers, Herbs, and Plants

I'm an herbalist. My love language is flowers. One of my ways of communicating my love and support to those in my community is to make them an herbal tea blend. Just had a baby? Dealing with depression? Lost a loved one? Coping with menopause? Just had surgery? Here is a blend! I hand deliver the herbal blends and instruct my recipients on how best to enjoy the goodness of the herbs.

While studying herbalism, I wondered if plants, flowers, and herbs were Heavenly Mother's idea. I wonder if she thought, "They are going to sometimes have menstrual cramps! We need to put some cramp bark in the Garden!" I marvel at the way flowers, herbs, and plants bring joy and delight to the senses and can support our physical bodies during the many challenges that mortality can bring. I wonder if this is Her way—one of the many ways—in which She nurtures us both temporally and spiritually for this sojourn on the earth.

Ashli Carnicelli

Education

The curriculum we've been sent to learn
is the geography of one another's hearts
the meter of sorrow and laughter
the histories of replenishment and drought
the solutions of compassion and hope
and the equations of grace and communion

I think my Mother taught me them before. I have only to remember.

Autumn Nelson

"But as it is written, Eye hath not seen, nor ear heard, neither have entered into the heart of man, the things which God hath prepared for them that love him."

1 Corinthians 2:9

Weaver

Our Mother: the spinner of creations weaving the web that is our home. Leaving messages for us in Her translucent writing, sticky to manage with our awkward fingers, but with our eyes opened, too radiant to ignore. She fell out of view before our eyes could behold Her. We might weep for Her loss, were it not for Her messages still entwined around our hearts. Our primal desires allow us to spin our own silk as we leap from the edge and trust the wind to carry us on our thin, fragile threads. Balloons in the sky, with no jubilant colors, but the joy in our hearts; Hoping to find a more permanent, eternal, solid perch. Find the strands that lead back to Her heartstrings, and in Her image we are found and whole, Her life giving us holy purpose, feeding us, nurturing us and as we partake, we become one with Her. Spinning and weaving worlds without number and lives without end, Creatress, Seamstress, Weaver of Stars and Time, our Mother.

Kayla Gisseman

Freckles on the Face of my Mother

A dark, heavy blue blankets the sky.
Stars freckled across Her timeless face;
Omnipotent endlessness in the deep night.

Then there is light.
The dawn turns to day
And the warmth greets my face.

Are freckles just kisses from angels?
Perhaps they are Mother's.
Adorning my face with constellations
Because She knows how I adore Hers.

Ashley Lauren Workman

The Portal

The womb:
a temple,
a sacred cocoon bridging
divine and mortal worlds
wherein a spirit transitions
from the realm of God
to the realm of mankind,
memorizing
the mother's heartbeat,
while also hearkening
to the parting wisdom
of Mother God.

                Jessica Woodbury

"This plan was presented to us while we lived as spirit children with our heavenly parents, who are the consummate examples of a perfect husband and wife, father and mother. Oh, how we must have loved Them and wanted to be just like Them! Their perfect love for each other and for us is eternal, and They want us to have all that They have. We must have rejoiced when we heard of the plan that would open the way for us to become as They are, even though it meant leaving Their presence."

Brother Larry M. Gibson, counselor in Young Men general presidency, 2009-15[36]

Delivery Day

She releases the birds one
by one into the air where
they can be seen and heard and
loved.
She doesn't think the birds belong in
cages anymore where
it is small.
She thinks the birds will carry Her song.
She thinks we'll hear them.

Olivia Flinders

Gold Leaf

The Mother is gold
leaf and mountains,
the color of the moon
and sky,

Her sharp line
angles remind me
to build and rebuild.

The Mother is the bridge
to winter, whispering
that Jesus came
through birth,
through Mary.

In spring her echoes
of a poet remind me
my children come
through me,
but are not
me.

I am the bow
sending them
forth to make
their own way
swift and far.

The Mother is the glacier
roots beneath my
house, reminding me
they intersect
and weave.

She is an artist,
tying words, and paint,
and hearts together,
building something new
every day of November.

Her own arrow
forever in many directions.

Rachel Hunt Steenblik

Sacred Alignment

Hanna Choi

Naming God

Poets are Namers
they title and describe and claim the world

I write poetry about God
and I give Them names

She is the God Who Sees Me
He is Father Love
She is Mother Earth
She is Rest
He is Protection
He is Forever
She is Progression
She is Upward, He is Onward
He is Here, and She is Now
They are Love Teacher
Heart-Healer
Hand-Holder

God Who Carries Me
Mama Divine
Father of My Soul
Warm Embrace
Light Embodied
Holy Place
Pillar of Wisdom
My Strength and Eben-ezer
Eternity and Everlasting

And remembering that God is the greatest Namer of us all, I suppose I could call Them "Poet" too.

Autumn Nelson

Pieta

Megan Geilman

Longtime renowned Utah artist and painter Lee Udall Bennion is cast as Mary in this reinterpretation of Michelangelo's Pietà. Replacing the body of Christ with a slaughtered sheep makes real the ties between Old Testament practices, hopes and beliefs, and the passion of the Christ. Bennion's mature stature connects to Heavenly Mother while challenging Michelangelo's famous notion that Mary should be eternally young.

8

Influences From Beyond

"President Harold B. Lee stated, "We forget that we have a Heavenly Father and a Heavenly Mother who are even more concerned, probably, than our earthly father and mother, and that **influences from beyond** are constantly working to try to help us when we do all we can."

Mother in Heaven essay, paragraph 4

"On a particularly difficult day, or sometimes a series of difficult days, what would this world's inhabitants pay to know that heavenly parents are reaching across those same streams and mountains and deserts, anxious to hold them close?"

Elder Jeffrey R. Holland[37]

Reaching

Our Mother loves us! She can reach us. Does that make your heart sing with joy? How can you feel your Mother reaching for you?

McArthur Krishna

This Doctrine is True

I recently had an experience when I was walking my 2-year-old in her stroller. Suddenly, my whole body was covered with goosebumps and I received a confirmation that this doctrine of Heavenly Mother IS true. This sacred experience led me to know with every fiber of my being that our Mother in Heaven is real, that She loves us, that She is involved in our daily lives and is reaching to us from across the veil in seemingly ordinary moments.

Ashli Carnicelli

Help From Above

As mothers, we feel the weight of raising our children. Knowing that we have help from above might be the most comforting thought of Motherhood. When I'm on my knees praying for my children, whether for guidance & direction or comfort & peace, Heavenly Mother comes forward. I feel Her presence so strongly when it comes to my children. Mother to mother, I feel Her love, Her compassion and strength. It is very clear to me that our Heavenly Mother cares for each of us and understands our feelings as a mother.

Cassia Nielsen

Mess

My soul
Is a woven creation
And when I'm sorrowful,
It unravels.
My insides knot
And they coil.
Until I am
A mess.
My Heavenly family
Detangle the stress
And when They are done
The Mother weaves me back together.

Ashley Lauren Workman

"For can a woman forget her sucking child, that she should not have compassion on the son of her womb? Yea, they may forget, yet will I not forget thee, O house of Israel."

1 Nephi 21:15

Mother, Where Art Thou?

I have read the ancient books
Searching for your name
Tracing every line on every page
Imagining your face

I hear echoes of your voice
In the silence of the night
As I strain to see your shadow
In the stories of so long ago

Chorus 1
Are you the binding on each page?
Are you the thread that ties
All humankind through every age?
Are you the spaces in between
Above, around, beneath?
Mother where art thou?

Were you there when it began
In the garden, near the tree?
The architect of Eden's door
For Eve and all humanity?

Chorus 2
Are you the cradle and the grave?
Are you the hand that lifts
All living things to higher ways?
Are you the soil and the rays?
The blossom and the waves?
Mother, where are thou?

Bridge
I long to see reflections
Of my grander self
I hunger for the possibilities
Your sons and daughters kneeling
Pleading for your revealing
We could use a mother now
Mother, where art thou?

Repeat Chorus 1

Julie de Azevedo Hanks

Seeing Her

Amanda Landeen

The Soft Spaces Between Heaven and Earth

She dwells in the inbetweens
the space between a smile and a tear
the floating air between heaven and earth
the moment of suspension before water hits water
in a great big waterfall of
Her existence
streaming down the canyon
carving rocks out
centimeter by centimeter over
millions of eons
making more space for Her
beyond the invisibles.

Olivia Flinders

The Gatherer

I am the one who calls you home
Come here, my lamb, come here
I sweep you into my fold with arms curving like the bows of boats, the shafts of canyons, the beams of the moon
All creation is within my grasp and my arms encompass the great expanse of the universe
I pluck you from your waste places, your deserts and solitudes
Your loneliness and sick beds
The shame of your secret corners
I carry you in the belly of my apron
In my center, in my heart of hearts, under the wing of my breath
Rest in my basket, this basin of ease
Behold the fruits of my gathering, the reds, the blues, the greens and yellows

The rough and smooth, bonded and free
The large and small, holy and unholy
The beloved and the friendless
All ye are beloved unto me
You are Mine
I call you
I know your name
remember Mine

        Autumn Nelson

Reminder

In 1909, the First Presidency taught that "all men and women are in the similitude of the universal Father and Mother, and are literally the sons and daughters of Deity."

I keep this taped to my mirror, to remind myself each morning that every single person I interact with, whether pleasant or unpleasant, is a son or daughter of God. Their behavior has no bearing upon how I see them and how I treat them—they are my spirit siblings!

Ashli Carnicelli

She Wept

June 25, 2020: This piece was created amidst the Black Lives Matter uprising of 2020 and ongoing protests for racial justice. These events also occurred during a global pandemic in which hundreds of thousands of people were (and continue to) suffering and dying.

I started this piece with the intent to display my own sorrow over the condition of the world. As I painted, I felt Her weeping with me, and it morphed into a depiction of Her divine sorrow.

Sometimes I wonder how She manages the sadness She must feel as She sends Her children to earth, knowing the oppression and pain that they are bound to face. I wonder how She feels anything but an overload of mom anxiety and sorrow as She watches Her children fighting, suffering, and hurting one another. I wonder if She ever feels too far from us. If She ever wishes She could bridge the distance between Her and the children that so desperately need Her comfort.

I don't know how She does it, but I can't imagine any other act requiring more strength and resilience than being The Divine Mother of all these imperfect, precious, mortal souls.

Natalie Cosby

The Truth

She is the one you
must tell the truth to
when She asks how you are.
When you start crying
you are safe in Her arms.
She scoops you to Her home
makes you tomato and mayo sandwiches
with fruit grown close to the earth.

    Rachel Hunt Steenblik

"I believe that every man, woman, and child has felt the call of heaven at some point in his or her life. Deep within us is a longing to somehow reach past the veil and embrace Heavenly Parents we once knew and cherished."

Elder Dieter F. Uchtdorf[38]

Solace from The Mother

~

Feel the wind, and feel me.
Hear the waves, and hear me.
The wind dances and plays.
The waves are constant, soothing, and sure.
Hear the birds sing, and know that I sing to you as well.
Feel the warmth of the sun, and feel the warmth of my love for you.
See the tree before you?
It is little, but sturdy,
And I have every confidence in this little tree.
It is out here
growing strong in the wind,
Near the waves,
Welcoming birds

And flourishing in the sunlight.
Chin up, my little beachcomber.
You are yet little, but sturdy,
And you are growing right where you need to be.
You have all my love.

I penned this poem on April 3rd, 2020, but these words did not feel like my own. I was seeking comfort during some dark moments, in a most peaceful place. This is something that has stuck with me since, and I'd love it if this could bring solace to others as well.

Chelsea Echols

Miscarriage

She holds my baby in Her arms
because I never got to

1 in 3, She told me
A statistic that sounded like mine—
She knows my pain

I hold the children you lost
Because I cannot hold the children I lost

Channing Olivia Hyde

Wildflower

In this arid place
She nurtured my roots
underground

And one day
I emerged
through the Dust

And I bloomed
into Her flower
cultivated by

the soft hands
of the Love
of God

McCall Char

Letters

The author Elizabeth Gilbert has a daily practice of writing letters to herself from love.

Heavenly Mother is synonymous with love. On days when I am struggling, I imagine what She would write to me. Perhaps this:

Dear One,

It is okay to be still. Take a deep breath in. Hold it. Now breathe out. That's it. You do not have to worry over all eternity. There is only now. I am ever present with you. Lay down your burdens. They have been carried already. Let your burden be Light.

All my love,
Your Mother

Jennie Loomis

Amber Lanning

With Me

She is with me in my miscarriages.
She understands and I don't even have to explain.
I don't have to say too little or worry if I say too much.
I don't even have to say it right or give all the backstory.
All of the probing questions—not from Her.
She's gentle and kind and a presence of overwhelming, complete love. It feels safe, warm, familiar and whole.
Enough. Her presence tells me that I am enough.
To Her, I say the same.
I don't have to shield Her from my pain and heartbreak.
There's no pretending to be strong and me searching for the right things to say to lessen Her discomfort.
She understands without words
The things only my heart can say.
And that is enough.

Emily Roundy

Close and Personal

In my patriarchal blessing it says, "I bless you that you will always have a close personal relationship with your mother and continue to have the love that you do now." I realized one day this was referring to my Heavenly Mother.

How can you develop a "close, personal relationship" with your Mother in Heaven?

Kelli Green

Connecting to Her

Acknowledging Godhood within us connects us to Her. One practical way I feel closer to my Heavenly Mother is by spending time in the temple. I gain this eternal perspective—remembering that where I've been is Her child before I came to mortality. We have the privilege of women blessing us in the temple during the Initiatory—this puts us in touch with our highest divine Mother.

Shima Baughman

Char Weiler

Mothering Through the Hard Moments With Heavenly Mother

Mothering three strong-willed, feisty, highly-opinionated daughters is not for the faint-hearted. Whenever I find myself overwhelmed with a particular mothering challenge or conundrum, I pause and remember this beautiful promise from the wise Relief Society general president, Jean Bingham:

> "Do you think our Heavenly Parents want us to succeed? Yes! They want us to succeed gloriously. And do you think They will help us? Absolutely!"

I've discovered that when I'm stuck—not knowing what to do to help my daughters navigate the countless challenges of earthly life—if I turn my thoughts upward to Heavenly Mother, I am often flooded with motherly inspiration . . . an insightful book to read, a counselor to talk to, a scripture to share, a friend to connect with, a conversation to be had, an experience to make happen. Mothering while remembering Heavenly Mother is so, so much better.

Bethany Brady Spalding

My Place

I crave the silence and peace
because I can find you there.

On this journey
I fight to quiet my storm
and sometimes
I glimpse your face.
A frame of deep lines and consuming love.

My children look to me
while their storms rage.
I am their place
For calm, for rest, for love.

Because you are my Mother
I know
that you are my place.

A balm for my wounds
A gentle strength

Calling me to expand
Breathing deep within me.

You are my place
for steadiness, for joy.
You are
my center, my form.

My Mother.

                Blakelee Ellis

Heavenly Mother Bearing Gifts

~

Michelle Gessell

Unseen

I fell down on my knees, sobbing
everything was overwhelming
I didn't know what I was seeking
I paused to feel what I was feeling

I felt unseen

I can't do this anymore
The laundry, the sink full of dishes
My back is so sore
I miss dreams, miss even my wishes

I sat down and closed my eyes
I was going to try to meditate
As I tried to even my breath, all I thought
was about what nobody could appreciate

Can somebody see me?
Am I worth nothing?
What do I do all day?
Can't they see I am bursting?

I just want to feel seen

Then it hit me.
It came like a small wave,
I started to finally see
all the things She must have given me

Dear Mother in Heaven,
I'm sure you can see me
I am so sorry that I never learned
to know you and to truly see

Dear Mommy in Heaven,
Maybe that's the missing piece
I need to learn to see you
In order to feel seen

Camilla Alves

Mother's Blessing

Mother breaks bread at our table
distributing every piece to every yearning hand
We close our palms around the sponge
and close our eyes in prayer
She eases our gaping hunger with Her milk
our mouths wide open, searching for Her
She fills us with warmth and power

I used to describe feeling the spirit like
warm milk trickling down my throat and
into my chest
It was before I knew Mother, and before I knew
milk
I think She was there all along
nourishing me.

Olivia Flinders

Sending My Baby Home

I have always loved you I said
You are part of my heart my dear
I know you are dying, you know it too
Although my heart is heavy, I do not fear

Heavenly Mother is near

I hold you close and breathe you in
I promise I will find you again
I have knowledge and hope in Christ
A spirit that surrounds with sweet refrain

Heavenly Mother is near

As the tears fall and I whisper
You will never truly leave me
Eternal families include you
Miraculous reunions shall be

Heavenly Mother is near

As She takes you from my arms
And your body falls still in mine

I sob with missing you already
Heavenly Mother whispers "she is fine

"I will hold her close
And keep her safe
Like I always do with you
My daughter, my warrior
Be brave, valiant and true
And one day I'll give your baby
Back to you
I am always here
Forever near
My daughter dear
Cry and grieve, I hold you too
Feel my love surrounding you

Your Heavenly Mother is near"

           Lorraine Pemberton

By Proxy

My Mother cannot be with me right now. I had to leave Her behind to journey on my own. But like any (fairy) God-Mother, She sends me gifts and messages along the way. My favorites are Her messengers. Her directions and love come to me in the form of proxy mothers, sprinkled on my path.

What women in your life help you feel the love of your Heavenly Mother?

Autumn Nelson

9

Connection

"Latter-day Saints direct their worship to Heavenly Father, in the name of Christ, and do not pray to Heavenly Mother."

Mother in Heaven essay, paragraph 5

Connection

Let us be clear. The Gospel Topics essay teaches this principle of prayer. However, we are commanded to have a relationship with Jesus Christ and we don't pray to Him either. But we know that our Mother is "reaching" for us. How can you connect with Her? Can you feel it when you consider the gift of Her Son, Jesus Christ? Can you feel it in the scriptures when it says, "A hen gathered her chicks . . ." Can you feel it?

McArthur Krishna

Calling Home

When I pray to Heavenly Father, I believe I'm talking to both Heavenly Father AND Heavenly Mother. When I "call home" through prayer, Heavenly Father doesn't have the receiver to His ear—He has me on speakerphone because Mom, the Holy Ghost and Jesus want to hear me too!

Ashli Carnicelli

Uncovering Heaven

Anne Clark

Confession

As a little child, I would leave my bedroom door open every night because I knew my mom would come and shut it as she did her bedtime rounds. I could have shut it myself and saved Mom the trouble, and I certainly would have gone to sleep earlier, less bothered by the hallway light pouring in. But there was something so sweet about feeling her ever-watchful eye, unfailingly delivering this last ritual of maternal care as I lay in bed drifting between degrees of consciousness.

How do I leave my door open so that my Heavenly Mother can come in and show Her love to me?

Autumn Nelson

Gifts

"Mom, I put a flower in the sea and gave it to Heavenly Mother!"

That flower was the gift my young daughter thought to offer her Divine Mother in a moment of joy near the ocean.

Do you sometimes think of Heavenly Mother in moments of beauty and happiness as my daughter did?

What symbolic gifts of gratitude or love can you choose to give to your Eternal Mother?

Would they be gifts of service to Her children, bearing witness of Her and Her Son, or developing Her attributes within you? What other unique gifts can you think to offer Her?

Jessica Woodbury

Greeting

How beautiful you are
How magical you must be
To have smitten me
With no formal
Or proper
Introduction

Emily Roundy

Letters With Mother

If you were to write a letter to Heavenly Mother, what would you say? What would you tell Her about? What questions would you ask? How would She answer you?

STEP 1 Take a moment to breathe deeply and allow yourself to be present. Say a prayer, if you'd like, and ask for the Spirit to guide you in receiving what you need through this exercise today.

STEP 2 In a journal or on a piece of paper, start by writing, "Dear Heavenly Mother" or another name that resonates for you. Write a letter to Her, pouring out your heart, desires, and questions.

STEP 3 Once that is complete, take some deep breaths. On the reverse side of the paper, start by writing, "Dear [your name]."

Write a response to your letter, as if Heavenly Mother is responding to you. What do you feel She would say in response? Tune in to your intuition and allow your thoughts and inspiration to flow freely as you write, opening up to receiving the messages that would be most supportive for you at this time.

STEP 4 When you are finished, perhaps you would like to close this exercise with another prayer, or you may choose to sit in a moment of gratitude for what you have received. Repeat this exercise as often as desired.

Megan Watson

A Mother's Womb

Dylan Landeen

Acrostic

Hope is in short supply.
Everything is in turmoil as I search for an
Anchor in the storm.
Very faint, a spiritual whisper brushes my heart,
Easy to miss if I'm not paying attention:
"No hate, no enmity.
Love only.
You will change things that
Most people would ignore."
Outside, my eyes are drawn to look up,
Trees frame my view of the clear sky.
Her sacred influence in the sunshine
Extends peace and calm, and
Restores my soul.

Trina Caudle

"We too can anticipate that when the time comes for us to step through the veil of mortality, leaving our failing and pain-filled bodies behind, we will see the loving smile and feel the welcoming embrace, not only of our Heavenly Parents and of the Savior, but also of our loved ones who will greet us in full vigor, full remembrance, and full love."

Sister Chieko N. Okazaki, counselor in Relief Society general presidency, 1990-97[39]

Her Brightness

It's like thunder and lightning
you see it before you
hear it
you feel it before
you see it.
Water drops one by one in
a different colored sky—
a darker and holier one—
you know Her before She happens.

When She happens,
everything is changed.
Soaked in Her brightness,
showered in Her glory,
damp soil and fresh hearts
(and starts)
ready for beginnings.

Olivia Flinders

Supply and Demand

She meets us at our hunger,
our anger, our sadness.
She makes, and makes,
and makes, and gives.

    Rachel Hunt Steenblik

Anita Schley

Mothering Support

At 2:30 a.m. I snuggled my daughter in our faded rocker, willing away my resentment and exhaustion. Weary in both body and spirit, I imagined myself hopping in the minivan and driving into the darkness. *Motherhood is one of my most important roles*, I thought, *and I am failing at it.*

I thought a desperate and incoherent prayer. *I need help. I need to be understood.* In that moment, I felt Her presence in the room with certainty. I knew I had a Mother who knew me, guided me, and supported me in my own journey of motherhood.

Lorren Lemmons

Whole Food

The older I get, the more I crave
balanced, complete nutrition.
Food in its most natural state.

Just like my aging body,
my wisening soul feels the deficiency
in a processed diet.

Body and soul thirst and hunger for whole food—
Untainted, unprocessed—in its most essential form.

I have eaten the grains of my forebearers
sifted and ground down, baked into
reliably uniform brown loaves-the
loaves that have fed me for decades.

But Wisdom beckons me to Her garden.
  Verdant and vibrant,
filled with green swoops, yellow curves,
  Overflowing with orange and red orbs.

Oh, the colors! The shapes and sizes!
The glorious variety of fruit and seed.

I stand in wonder at the offering of
    Mother Earth.
In awe of the breadth and the bounty,
It is delicious and desirable,
Inviting and enticing.

I will eat of Her fruit.
I will partake of Their fullness,
I will be nourished with loaf and leaf
And I will be Whole.

>   Rebecca Young

"Of the Rock that begat thee thou art unmindful, and hast forgotten God that formed thee."

Deuteronomy 32:18

Guided Meditation

~

Go outside and sit under a tree. Take a few moments to breathe deeply and allow yourself to be present.

Meditate on the following symbols, or anything else which comes to you as you enjoy the energy of the tree:

How is Heavenly Mother like this tree? What attributes do they share?

How is Heavenly Mother like the roots of this tree? Imagine you have roots growing from the bottom of your feet, deep into the center of the earth. How can your Mother's love for you help you feel anchored and grounded?

Feel the tree with your hand. How is Heavenly Mother like the trunk and branches of this tree? How can you invite Her support into your life even more?

If you could cut a cross-section of the tree, you would see many growth rings which tell the life story and age of the tree. Imagine you can examine a cross-section and all the growth rings representative of your relationship with Heavenly Mother over eons of time before you came to Earth. What story would the growth rings tell? If Heavenly Mother could tell you of your story together, what would She say to you?

Notice any leaves or fruit or blossoms on the tree. How is Heavenly Mother like leaves and fruit and blossoms? Ponder Her attributes as a divine creator. How are her creations a blessing? How can you bless others with what you create throughout your life?

Some additional ideas for meditations:

How is Heavenly Mother like flowing water?

How is Heavenly Mother like the moon?

How is Heavenly Mother like a glacier, slowly carving out a mountain?

How is Heavenly Mother like a flower?

Megan Watson

Krystal Root Andrew

My Mother's Love

My Mother speaks to me through a child's laugh.
She whispers to me through the gentle breeze.
She sings to me through the bird's call at dawn.
She paints me pictures in the sunset.
She embraces me on a warm summer day.
She writes me love notes in the stars.
She plays with me in the waves of the sea.
She kisses me with the gentle rain.
My Mother sends Her love.

Britt Manjarrez

Cucumber Lime Agua Fresca

This recipe reminds me of Heavenly Mother for several reasons: The fresh, refreshing taste brings me joy, and connecting with Heavenly Mother refreshes me and brings me joy. This drink also reminds me of long lunches at a restaurant with close friends sipping refill after refill, and I know Heavenly Mother joys in me connecting with kindred friends and having inspired conversations. To me, this drink also represents diversity as I discovered a version of it at Zao Asian Cafe but found the recipe online as a Mexican drink. Finally, the spring-green color reminds me of creation, and I think of Heavenly Mother as a divine creator.

Cucumber Lime Agua Fresca
(Adapted from a recipe found at Mexicoinmykitchen.com)

2 cucumbers (about 3 cups once chopped)
1/2 cup lime juice (about 4-8 limes)
6 cups water, separated

2/3 cup sugar (or 1 teaspoon liquid stevia—I use SweetLeaf brand)
3 cups ice
Lime and cucumber slices for garnish if desired

Peel cucumbers and chop them into chunks. Place in a blender. Add lime juice, 2 cups water, and sugar or stevia. Process until smooth. Pour through a strainer into a large drink pitcher, pressing down with the back of a large spoon to extract as much liquid as possible. Discard the pulp. Add the other 4 cups water and 3 cups ice cubes. Refrigerate for an hour. Taste and add more sweetener or water as desired. To serve, place some lime or cucumber slices in glasses if desired. Enjoy! Makes a little more than a half-gallon.

Becky Edwards

The idea of having a Heavenly Mother is obvious to me. I am a girl who will someday become a woman. It says in the scriptures that I was made in God's image—and I'm not a man—so it must be that I was created in Her image. I come from Her! I love knowing this.

> Isla Rose Carnicelli, age 9

Grandmother's Wisdom

Listen to the song "She'd Say" by Andy Grammer. The song references Grammer's mother who passed away a few years before his daughter was born and conveys the things he believes his mother would most want her granddaughter to know. You will hear a Zulu phrase, "Ngiyamkhumbula umama wami," in the background which translates as, "I miss my mom."

After listening, reflect on what words of wisdom Heavenly Mother might want included if a song like this were written referencing Her. Notice how you feel as you consider Her desire for a relationship with you.

Moriann Barker

Primary Songs

One of the ways I connect with and honor Heavenly Mother is to change the words of church songs to align more fully with our restored doctrine of Heavenly Parents. For example, I like to sing, "I am a child of God and They have helped me here," to my sons.

What songs would you change to include Her?

Kristine Hoyt

Short Poetry

Consider writing a short poem with one-word lines starting with "Heavenly Mother is . . ." You may try adaptations such as "Heavenly Mother's heart, hands, arms, eyes, or ears are . . ."

Here is an example:

Heavenly Mother is
Nurturing
Cherishing
Creating
Healing
Holding
Safe

Becky Edwards

10

Eternal Prototype

"Indeed, as Elder Rudger Clawson wrote, 'We honor woman when we acknowledge Godhood in her **eternal Prototype**.'"

Mother in Heaven essay, paragraph 5

Be Ye Therefore Perfect

As Heavenly Mother is my eternal prototype, this does not point to earthly perfection by any means. When Christ said, "Be ye therefore perfect, even as your Father which is in heaven is perfect" (Matthew 5:48), the same applies to women to be perfect as our Heavenly Mother is perfect. The word "perfect" is best translated as "whole." We can only be whole and holy through The Holy One. We can look to Heavenly Mother as our eternal prototype and realize this potential through Jesus Christ.

Ashli Carnicelli

My Prototypes

~

Evelyn: serves always. Tawnia: cares for all children. Emily: without guile. Mindy: creative with her hands. Clarissa: loves puppies. Laurel: eye for color. Michelle: never quits. Amanda: appreciates nature. London: protective of LGBTQ youth. Naomi: family loyalty. Helen: fearless testimony of Christ. Sarah: pure faith. Theresa: an open home. Beth: adventurer. Marisol: long-term friendship. Jane: community focus. Kristi: consistent ministering. Kelly: kind and tender heart. Liz, Allie, Rosemary: empowering women. Marci: encouragement. McArthur, Ashli: teamwork and unity.

Heavenly Mother: all of this, and more, in a glorified state.

Trina Caudle

My Role Model

How many of us growing up wanted to be a superhero? A rock star? How many of us hung pictures on our wall of inspiring women?

The truth is, our most perfect feminine model is our Mother in Heaven. When we look for the model of our lives as women of faith, we know what is of true value. As Heavenly Mother is cherished, so am I. As Heavenly Mother works on the plan for our lives, so will I. As Heavenly Mother works with Heavenly Father, so will I. As Heavenly Mother loves her children, so will I. As Heavenly Mother became a god, so will I.

McArthur Krishna

Our Mother's Names

~

Sage Gallagher

"This divine entreaty is consistent with the fact that, as begotten children of heavenly parents, we are endowed with the potential to become like them, just as mortal children may become like their mortal parents."

President Russell M. Nelson[40]

Childproof

In the afternoon we practice quiet time
Temporarily parting ways
My children play and sleep and read
Nearby I peek and sip and breathe
Practicing their independence
Within the reach of their parent.

I try to practice my own quiet time
So I may "be still and know"
While here, I learn and stumble and grow
Nearby They await and peer and cheer
Trying to become like my Parents
Within reach of the Atonement.

Ashley Lauren Workman

Model

As an engineer by trade, I know the importance of having a prototype—an original model—when designing something. A prototype is a first full scale and fully functional form of a new type of design or construction. I love the idea that Heavenly Mother is our eternal prototype as human beings.

Lisa Page

"To sow in the Spirit means that all our thoughts, words, and actions must elevate us to the level of the divinity of our heavenly parents."

Elder Ulisses Soares[41]

Stretch Marks

Mother's heart
stretches over
all Her children.

Her stretch marks
are bigger than Grace's.

And just like Grace,
Mother says, "I don't mind.
You're worth it."

I made this drawing from a photo of my daughter Grace's stretch marks in her first pregnancy.

Becky Edwards

Green

Green.
The color of life.
Of leaves on the Tree.
Like the Divine Mother,
Who helped give life to us all.

In Eden, what else
Would they choose, except
Vivid green fig leaves,
Adorned at the inception of mortal life.
The first semblance of clothing
Dressed just
as a mother
would dress her baby.

I reach my arms heavenward,
Seeking Her face.
She teaches me
Words to speak,
Works to act,
showing me how
I can grow up to be
Just like Her.

Sadie Hanna

Attributes

I grew up Catholic. I am a convert to The Church of Jesus Christ of Latter-day Saints. I grew up with the concept of Mary, the mother of Jesus Christ, as the divine feminine prototype to aspire to. When I want to learn more about who my Heavenly Mother is, I study about Mary in the scriptures. What attributes does she share with our Heavenly Mother? Dignity and strength are two that stand out to me. What stands out to you?

Ashli Carnicelli

Daughter's Gift

~

When my daughter Eva was 14, she drew this picture of me holding her as a baby, and gave it to me for Mother's Day. It was drawn on regular paper with a number two pencil. On my collar and her blanket, she lovingly noted "Tess" and "Eva."

I keep it on my desk at work. When I see it, I wonder if my daily walk is a gift to my Heavenly Mother. Does she keep my actions, words, and thoughts in a special place on Her desk? Today, I will honor Heavenly Mother by letting my life be a gift to Her, one that She can proudly display.

Tracie Frost

Mother, Daughter, Sister, Friend

I often sit under
a cool shady tree

and I like to ponder
what you have taught me

you remind me of
our Mother in Heaven

you teach me wisdom
so lovingly

McCall Char

What Would Mother Do?

~

We sometimes see the acronym "WWJD" on jewelry or bumper stickers. It stands for "What Would Jesus Do?" and is a wonderful way to center ourselves in following the Savior's example. Likewise, asking "WWMD"—What Would Mother Do?—can center ourselves in following Her female, motherly example in addition to the Savior's. Consider pondering or journaling about the questions below.

- What might Heavenly Mother do in my situation?
- How do I see Heavenly Mother's hand in my life right now?
- How can I be Heavenly Mother's hands in blessing someone today?

Becky Edwards

Her Likeness

For years I had been searching
for my Mother's likeness in the mirror.
I never found it
until one day I heard Her say
"Daughter. How could you see me
if you know not who I am?
Seek.
And once you know me, I promise
you will see me there."

Jaylen Dodds Bohman

A Body Like Hers

Some of the most spiritual experiences happen at Zumba class. I have no professional training. No one would think much of my dancing. But when my feet move to the steps of the Samba or my hands twist to a South Asian beat, I feel alive. I feel like my Heavenly Mother's daughter. I chose to come here and have a body like Hers! I'm convinced She loves her body and I love mine too.

What helps you to love your body, which is made in Her image?

Angela Ricks

Mothers

I'm lucky to have a mom
whose love reflects Hers
who shows me glimpses
of what Mother is like
what She might feel

I'm lucky to have a mom who's missing Her too
who's desperate to find Her
to know Her
to love Her
who feels the injustices that surround us
and Her

I'm lucky to have a mom who cares for me
like She does
who shows me what it means to be a mother
like our Mother

I'm lucky to have my mom
and I'm lucky to have my Mother.

Channing Olivia Hyde

Teach Me Through the Light

Hanna Choi

"Have you ever been told you are just like your mother, or you have your father's smile, or all of your family have the same color of eyes? The physical characteristics that we inherit from our parents are obvious. The spiritual characteristics we inherit from our heavenly parents have to be developed."

President Elaine L. Jack, Relief Society general president, 1990-97; counselor in Young Women general presidency, 1987-90[42]

A Mirror to Her

Sending a child on a mission is both a joyful and excruciatingly painful experience for me and, I think, for most mothers. On one hand, there is so much to celebrate in their choice to serve and sacrifice in this way. There is comprehension of the tremendous growth that they will experience through the process, not just spiritually but in nearly every possible way.

Simultaneously, there is loss and grief. There is of necessity not only a physical separation for an extended length of time, but also less opportunity to communicate as frequently as a mother might desire. There is knowledge that growth comes with painful experiences and heartache. As a mother, I struggled with my instincts to protect and nurture and keep my son close, while knowing that he needed this more.

In the first days and weeks of my son's

mission, I thought often of our Heavenly Mother and Her courage and the possible conflict within Her as She let each one of us come to earth, knowing that there would be pain, separation, and loss, but also knowing the growth and joy that would come to us. It connected me to Her and to Her love for me as Her daughter. And it gave me the courage to be okay with the internal conflict over my son's mission.

Michal Thomas

She Fills Her Own Well

The Mother fortifies
Herself with rainbows,
trees, sunsets,
so She has something
to give us,
so She has something
to give Herself.

Rachel Hunt Steenblik

Mother

A couple of nights ago I couldn't sleep, and I was thinking about my sweet little 5-year-old girl who cried in my lap that day that "she wished she was an artist so she could make anything!" She was frustrated that her art wasn't as grandiose as she imagined and wished it to be. Instead of reaching for social media in the middle of the night, I wrote a little poem for her, something I hadn't done in about a decade:

Creation
There is no limit to creativity
No borders on love
There is no gate on imagination
Reach for the sky above
There is no wrong way to use a paintbrush
If painting from the heart.
So take what is inside you
And create—art.

Amanda Jenkins

"And then shall the angels be crowned with glory of his might, and the saints shall be filled with his glory, and receive their inheritance and be made equal with him."

D&C 88:107

Body Meditation

Take a shower or bath or just dress down to your comfort level. Your body has been patterned after our eternal Prototype. Female and Male, we were created like Them. Begin with gratitude and end with a statement of love for each part starting from your head down, gently dismissing negative thoughts that sneak up. Example: "I'm grateful for my eyes, for all they allow me to see, for the light that they take in, for the connection they provide when I look into another's, for the beautiful unique color they are. I love my eyes."

Scan your body and consider the job and the blessings of all your body parts: the head, the neck, the shoulders, the back, the breast, the loins, the legs, the feet . . . Try to be as thorough as you can.

All of you is good, worthy, and blessed. If you struggle to feel love for your body, ask God to share Their love for it with you. Repeat often.

Kate Gregory

Intuition

I think knowing Her is intuitive
You already know Her before you know Her
Then when you know Her
you know yourself.

        Olivia Flinders

Night After Night

Night after night
I care for my baby
A mother constant
And loving
I walk down the hall
Open the door
And lay
My weary body
down
She is here
And tucks me in
With a soft smile
Full of eternal
Tenderness
The Mother cares
for Her child,
Even as I care
for mine

McCall Char

Reflection

Every good woman (and I know an abundance of them)
Is a reflection of Her, She is the embodied form of every one of their gifts and virtues
Eve, Sarah, Hagar, Rebekah, Rachel, Leah, Deborah, Abish, Mary, Joan, Emma, Margaret, Carol, Wendy, Patricia, Sharon, Chieko, Malala, Rachel, Kathryn, my mother, grandmother, me, (and many many more).

Autumn Nelson

She Came to Me First in a Rainbow

My painting is an attempt to encapsulate my first experience with my Heavenly Mother in a portrait. I was between ten and twelve years old and had just had some sort of argument with my parents, and had taken my broken and misunderstood heart out to sit on the front porch of my home. I honestly do not remember where I might have heard the concept that there may even be a Mother in Heaven besides the beloved hymn O, My Father by Eliza R. Snow, but as I was sitting there in my sadness, I had the urge to talk to Her. I wanted to pray to her but that felt like it might be a sin, so I prayed to God as I knew Him then and asked permission to speak to my Mother. I poured my heart out to Her and was wrapped in a peace and warmth that was new to me. I felt safe and seen. As I wiped away my tears, I looked up to see a large and intense rainbow arching the sky in front of me. This was a profound moment for me and the first of many to come.

I have since learned that for me, She comes in the way I need to see her at that moment. She is mutable and infinite in Her forms and methods of support, just like earthly mothers must be for the needs of their individual children. Hence, I have depicted Her here as she felt to me at the moment I first remember meeting Her; multicolored, age a reflection of my youth, delicate and intensely present. She has come to me in many other ways throughout my life.

Kirsten Beitler

My Reflection

"I look like a mom," my 5 year old said
As she looked in the mirror
At her curls, lip gloss, and carefully picked out shoes.
"No!"—my internal voice
"You look like a fancy girl, a movie star, a queen!"
As I looked in the mirror at a tired ponytail, chapstick, and an old T-shirt.
But out loud, instead—"what do moms look like?"
"They have hair styles, and are beautiful, and wear high heels," was her response as she looked admiringly at herself. And at me.
Looking like a mom.
Not an insult,
A compliment.
When did Mother become something small

Or unimportant?
Is that a reflection of my Eternal Mother?
Or of my Earthly Mother?
Or of myself.
Mother.
Tired, but triumphant
Maybe ragged, but always regal
Not an insult,
A compliment.

Amanda Jenkins

11

Sacred Knowledge

"As with many other truths of the gospel, our present knowledge about a Mother in Heaven is limited. Nevertheless, we have been given sufficient **knowledge** to appreciate the **sacredness** of this doctrine."

Mother in Heaven essay, paragraph 6

Remembering

I grew up Catholic. I am a convert to The Church of Jesus Christ of Latter-day Saints. I grew up with the concept of Mary, the mother of Jesus, as the divine feminine prototype to aspire to. As an investigator, we sang "O My Father" to begin a Sunday School lesson. I turned to a friend beside me, pointed to the lyrics and whispered, "We have a Heavenly Mother?!" She said "Yes!" All the celestial bells went off in my head. *YES! I KNEW IT!* It felt like remembering.

As an adoptee, I know all too well that knowing where you come from helps you to truly understand who you are and who you have the potential to become. With this doctrine, I discovered my identity as a spirit daughter of God. I know who I am. I know whose I am. And I know who I can become as I walk the covenant path and strive for exaltation. This knowledge has changed everything for me.

One of the most tender applications of knowing that we have a Heavenly Mother has been as I parent my four daughters. As I look into their eyes, I wonder how many of Her attributes they have. As I guide them with this knowledge, I believe it will instill in them a sense of inherent worth and divine dignity. I believe that this knowledge will guide their words, actions, and choices with the desired result being more loving, Christ-like behavior and a deep respect for others and for themselves.

Ashli Carnicelli

Starting Blocks

I was on the track and field team in high school—my event was running the stopwatch for the sprinters. I watched them settle onto the starting blocks with their feet at 45-degree angles, their weight on their hands to balance. Getting positioned on the starting block took longer than the actual races. If a runner was not solid on the block for the starting gun, they would launch onto their face instead of down the track on their feet.

After Elder Renlund's general conference talk in April 2022, I thought a lot about the Gospel Topics essay about Mother in Heaven. It seemed to say so little. I received the spiritual insight that the essay is our starting block, and too many people—including me—are not yet properly positioned and balanced on it to proceed down the track of receiving more understanding about Heavenly Mother.

I believe it will be a lifetime pursuit of studying the essay, the resources in the footnotes of the essay, and the scriptures to gain the light and knowledge I am seeking about Heavenly Mother. It will take a lifetime of emulating the Savior to become like Her. This race is not a short sprint, but the most strenuous distance race of my life. It is good to be secure on the starting block as I begin.

Trina Caudle

Where Do I Learn of the Sacred

I pray to my Father in Heaven and I ask, "Does my Mother exist? Does She love me? Does She care?" and the answer is a deep welling of YES.

McArthur Krishna

"Ask, and it shall be given you; seek, and ye shall find; knock, and it shall be opened unto you: for every one that asketh receiveth; and he that seeketh findeth; and to him that knocketh it shall be opened."

Matthew 7:7-8

Haven

She is the shelter
The safe space
The come as you are
The Christlike countenance
The one who desires to see
and know
you
Rather than telling you
Who She thinks you are.
She's the kindness
the captive audience
the fascinated scientist
who asks the questions
'What is it like to be you?'

No measuring stick
No checklist
No molds
Her standard is FAITH
Her standard is HOPE
Her standard is CHARITY
Without guile
Without shame
She only asks
That you are willing
to be seen.

                       Ashli Carnicelli

"I bear my witness that each woman is a beloved daughter of Heavenly Parents, and in this latter-day has been given the opportunity to be endowed with priesthood power that will help her achieve all her righteous desires and dreams."

President Jean B. Bingham, Relief Society general president, 2017-22[43]

Heavenly Mother Wisdom

James 1:5 says, "If any of you lack wisdom, let [them] ask of God, that giveth to all [humankind] liberally, and upbraideth not; and it shall be given [them]." I am so grateful that we can ask God our questions about Heavenly Mother. We can pray to God and ask for a connection with Heavenly Mother and that wisdom will be given to us.

Malinda Wagstaff

The Remembering Woman

∽

Sing, O ye Mountains
Rejoice, O ye foothills
My mother has begun to love herself again
and blossoms sprout about the crinkles of her
 eyes
her remembrance is the earth's renewal
wait and watch the world awaken under her
 feet

woman, it is the whole earth— joy harjo

How does remembering your Heavenly Mother change how you love yourself?

Autumn Nelson

Krystal Root Andrew

Divine Esteem

A lot of us are lost. I think there are a lot of women who don't know who they are. We have self-esteem—in the world, our self-worth is "you" and that's all that matters. I like to think that what we need is not self-esteem, it's "divine-esteem"— where are we in relation to the divine?

If you can actually articulate or feel: *I am a daughter of God, I am a daughter of a Heavenly Mother and Father and I can be just like Her. She's divine and she's a Queen and a Priestess and She has all of these powers AND She's watching over me.*

Isn't that so much better than "self-esteem"? Our Heavenly Father and Heavenly Mother are rooting for us and we are just like Them. We have Their attributes. Isn't that so much better than what the world has to offer? The world says, "You can just love yourself." I'd rather have God love me!

Shima Baughman

Understanding Them

Knowing that I have a Heavenly Father AND a Heavenly Mother to return to fills me with joy and makes me want to follow Jesus Christ and walk the covenant path even more. The gifts of eternal life, eternal families, exaltation are more than I can comprehend. But the thought of another gift—a celestial reunion and living in the presence of my Heavenly Mother—fills me with love and gratitude for the Savior!

Jesus Christ is the condescension of God. He is what we know of God. The more I follow Him, listen to Him speaking through the Holy Ghost, and study His word, the more I know and understand who my Heavenly Parents are.

Ashli Carnicelli

The Mother As a Tree

Perhaps ancient Israel honored Her
And saw Her in the trees,
Beheld Her as a tower
And preached beneath Her dancing leaves
With lofty branches and deep roots
Her first born as the born fruit
From Her: a fruitful tree of life.
"Asherah": their understanding of the Wife.

A logical interpretation
For a tree to be divine
For the tree to be a tower
(And the tower to be Thine,
For I have never failed to feel God's power
In the midst of a great grove.)
It's simple to see why they may have endowed Her
With an image of creation and growth.

Of course, it is just a symbol.
A way to understand.

But how soberingly beautiful
To imagine Her wooden hands,
In Her strong lumber
That shelters from the storm.
Strong enough for Her to carry
The first Spirit She had borne.

From budding blossom, fruit, to cross
One Mother's communion and another's loss
As a tree, She withstood the atoning tempest
As a tree, She held Her Son's body, lifeless
A presiding image of the sacrifice He made.
One that held Him before
The grave He overcame.

Perhaps the Israelites sought Her
With the image of a tree
But Her true image is in the daughters
Made like Her; you and me.

Ashley Lauren Workman

At A Glance

A mountain, my temple
A song, my prayer
A book, my searching
And She is there.

A child's grasp, my purpose.
A sister's heart, my care
A family's journey, my all.
She is everywhere.

Maddie Daetwyler

Looking Into the Eyes

~

In this world, we can become so caught up in the outer image of ourselves and others. Years ago, I realized that every time I crossed paths with another woman, I was making a snap judgment in my head. It only took me a split second to complete a comparison between myself and her. One day, I was getting ready to attend Time Out for Women and these beautiful words came into my mind from David Stendl-Rast:

> "Look at the faces of people whom you meet. Each one has an incredible story behind their face. A story you could never fully fathom."[44]

I resolved to NOT notice the physical body of those I would meet that day but only to look into their eyes and see their beautiful faces for who they really are—children of our Heavenly Mother and Father. It was a meaningful shift for me in the way I saw those around me and it helps me to see others as our Heavenly Parents see them.

Rebecca Young

Know

I say I think I'm tired
of learning sad things
I cannot.
Please,
no more.

She answers back quickly
with healing in Her wings
You must.
Please,
know more.

Olivia Flinders

Almighty

Stranded all alone
No place to call my home
One hears me
Every cry

I know your name
I feel its grace
Strength overcoming
The darkest parts in me
I am suddenly free

Oh, God, Almighty
How are you so wonderful
How are all your works
So incredible
After all you have done for me
Given me
Almighty

Cherish

I stand this very hour
Realizing your great power
Thought I was abandoned
Now I see

You cried all my tears
Through all of these years
And take time to hear my every plea

How are you so wonderful
Almighty

   Krystal Richey Barnes

Invitation

Looking for Her in the divine pattern, in the scriptures, in your life?
INVITE HER IN.
Perhaps this is the way it will happen. One at a time, in a quiet sacred
moment between the two of you, involving a new birth, and new life.
One at a time. Mother and child. Just the two of you.
Knock on the door that echoes of eternity.
Seek the love that came
before.
Invite.
And find.

Mandy Green

Evidence

As a mortal mother holds her baby,
After the crescendo of birth takes place,
The pains melt away.
What's left is the life she has made:
In itself, this creation is a testament
Of the mortal mother.

Because of the creosote,
The cherry blossoms,
The dandelions,
And the date palms
Because I can
And because I am

Because I know as a mortal mother does,
I know that immortal Mother was.

Ashley Lauren Workman

"I testify of loving Heavenly Parents."

> President Linda K. Burton,
> Relief Society general
> president, 2012-17[45]

My Mothers and I

Hong Kong, 2021: I honor Heavenly Mother through my works, firstly, by developing the gifts she's given me. I made my mom a drawing for Mother's Day when I was fourteen, and I practiced so that the next year's art would be better than the last. I made this latest drawing at age nineteen, and offer my improvement to Her.

Second, I work on my relationships with others. One of the most treasured joys of my life has been discovering Heavenly Mother alongside my mom. As we grow closer to each other and become successful in our works, we take comfort in the fact that She is always looking over our shoulders.

Eva J. Frost

Reaching for Her

It laps at the edge of my memory,
like reaching for a wave
that has already gone back out to sea.
Or the image of a flame in my mind's eye,
though the candle's already blown out.

I reach for the memory, but my hands return
    empty.
But I'm certain
that if I could just reach a bit farther
I would reach Her.

I reach for the memory
of a mother whispering over a cradle
"don't forget me down there."

With the encouraging and bittersweet smile
of a mother watching her child grow,
She hugs Her child tight to Her chest,
then slowly lets go.

Away, away, away

Her child travels.
Away from Her safe embrace
Away from the safety of the cradle
Away from every memory of Her.

To a place where Her child won't remember to miss Her.
To a place where Her child won't learn to speak of, or to Her.

Yet I am starting to see Her now.

It's an image so fleeting, yet so real.
The idea of Her taunts my memory and teases my recollection.
She is a dream I am trying hard to remember.

After 23 years, I have woken up, looked around, and realized,
something is wrong here.
I want my Mother near.

How have I not realized before
that I needed something more?

I need the softness of my Mother's smile and the twinkle in my Father's eyes.
I need Her strength and His power
I need both Their arms wrapped around me.

Somewhere at the edges of my memory, like tenuous mist disappearing in the dawn
I think I hear Her say,

"Remember how I rocked you to sleep, my child.
Remember my embrace.
Remember how I wiped away each tear you shed,
and remember how much I loved you."

"Know that I still rock you to sleep, my child.
Know my embrace.

Know that I'll wipe away each tear you'll ever
    shed,
and know how much I love you."

"I am still here" She says,
"I never went away.
And if you look for me,
you will find me.
I am in the stars, I am in the sunrise, and
I am in your countenance."

She was never lost,
We were.

But I am finding Her.

Laura Detweiler

Who Am I?

In 2020, I was struggling to support my student husband, homeschool my four children, find direction in my career, all while far away from family in a new area through a pandemic. I read a quote by President Nelson encouraging us to ask God to help us know who we really are. So I asked. And She was there. She had been there all along. Like remembering a song I knew once but hadn't thought of in years, my soul knew Her.

I asked God to show me who I really was, and They showed me Her.

Katie Jordan

Knock

Sincere hearts
Contrite Spirits
Find the warmth
Of their Parents

Ashley Lauren Workman

Longing

we can't find sleep
though it's been
hours
since the stars
revealed themselves
beyond the window

the two of us
homesick friends
longing
in the stillness
for Her

wishing
we could remember
what She looked like
and the way
She must have
loved us

tears
and words

spill out
in a prayer

and then it comes
softly

a whispered
promise
in the darkness

"you will know Her"

Lauren Madsen

Mother Love

Mother love is
Healing to my core
Connecting me with heaven
Creating heavenly connections with others
Comforting, holding me, and holding space for my pain
Peace-giving after dissonance
Nurturing and nourishing day and night
Recharging, refilling me in Her rest
Celebrating with me
Creating and helping me create with beauty, authenticity, and joy
Life-giving, vibrant, radiant
Radically inclusive, unconditionally loving
Laughing with joy and delight
Seeing and cherishing all of me
Trusting my journey, walking by my side

Filling me with her love for me
Healing and expanding my love for myself
  and for others
Like the Good Samaritan—
Healing salve, bandages, warm soup, and a
  hot soak
Laying on the grass on a sunny day soaking
  her in

Becky Edwards

"God is your father, He loves you, He and your Mother in Heaven value you beyond any measure. You are unique, one of a kind, made of the eternal intelligence which gives you claim upon eternal life. Let there be no question in your mind about your value as an individual. The whole intent of the gospel plan is to provide an opportunity for each of you to reach your fullest potential, which is eternal progression and the possibility of godhood."

President Spencer W. Kimball[46]

A Prayer

I said a prayer last night.
I said, God, thank you for seeing me
And for loving me through others
And God replied, and said:
Thank you for seeing me.

How have you felt Heavenly Mother's love through others? What can you do to better see Her influence in your life?

Eliza Peterson

When I Woke Up in the Dark

When I woke up
in the dark
in a foreign land
to my brother's death
and an impending birth
God cradled me
cried with me
and gave me drops
of milk and moon
to swallow.

The Mother helps me
carry my dead,
nesting their names
in Her large hands
before pressing them
against Her heart:
Hyrum,
Terri,
David,
Annie.

She says, *They are heavy,*
because they are golden.
She says, *I'm strong,*
and my memory is clear.
She says, *It's easier*
if we do it together.

Rachel Hunt Steenblik

12

Highest Aspiration

~

"As Elder Dallin H. Oaks of the Quorum of the Twelve Apostles has said, 'Our theology begins with heavenly parents. Our **highest aspiration** is to be like them'."

Mother in Heaven essay, paragraph 6

Women Need Divine Vision

What we need to do is keep the vision. Elder Oaks said in the Gospel Topics Essay, "Our theology begins with heavenly parents. Our highest aspiration is to be like them." If we think of our Heavenly Parents, then we have a model of who we want to become. For women, it is vital to know of our Mother in Heaven. As we consider who She is, we know who we can become.

McArthur Krishna

Becoming Like Her

My patriarchal blessing talks about having a mighty change of heart and going from being a woman of the world to a woman of Christ. Heavenly Mother is a woman of Christ. As I keep my covenants and live the law of sacrifice by putting off the natural man each day, the Lord can mold me and turn my heart away from the world, towards Him. This makes me more like Her.

Ashli Carnicelli

Mother Love, Self Love

～

You loving, adoring, cherishing me right where
 I am
is teaching me to better love myself right where
 I am.
You forgiving me so easily and thoroughly
is teaching me to forgive myself easily and
 thoroughly.

You seeing my good amidst my messiness
is teaching me to see my good amidst my
 messiness.
You celebrating my successes, large and small
is teaching me to celebrate my successes,
 large and small.

You trusting me
is teaching me to trust myself.
You meeting me right where I am
is teaching me to meet myself right where I am.

You are healing my relationship with me.
Thank you.

    Becky Edwards

"Sisters, I testify that when you stand in front of your heavenly parents in those royal courts on high and you look into Her eyes and behold Her countenance, any question you ever had about the role of women in the kingdom will evaporate into the rich celestial air, because at that moment you will see standing directly in front of you, your divine nature and destiny."

Elder Glenn L. Pace, Seventy[47]

"O ye house of Israel whom I have spared, how oft will I gather you as a hen gathereth her chickens under her wings, if ye will repent and return unto me with full purpose of heart."

3 Nephi 10:6

Heavenly Mother Galaxy

I see Her beauty in the mountains
Purple and Majestic.
I see Her grace in the clouds
White as her hair and Pure.
I feel Her radiance in the breeze
With the scent of flowers in the air.
And hear Her laughter like the bluebird's song.

I see Her in the Galaxy
Shining like the stars.
In the river waters
Strong and Carving a new path.
I felt Her warm embrace at the birth of a child.
Saying goodbye
as I said hello.

There is Her beauty all around us.
White and Pink, Yellow and Blue.
In the music and the sunshine.
In the person that offers a smile.
In the mother that laughs with her child.

I see Her strength.
I feel Her calmness.
I can hear Her lullaby.
Listen and Seek and
you will find Her too.

        DeAnna Christensen

A Mother's Joy

I'm running back and forth through
A temporary space,
Chasing my growing boy on tip-toes
As he excitedly bounces down the hallway
The hollow pitter patter bounces such happy
   notes against the walls.
They echo resounding notes of joy around my
   soul.
What moments these are
That fill me up even until I pour over

Does a Heavenly Mother
Have moments like these?
What moments fill Her heart,
Like the sound of a toddler's happy feet?
Does She feel overwhelming joy
From each
Of our clumsy stumbles toward growth?

Ashley Lauren Workman

God's Love

～

The most powerful experience I've had with our Heavenly Mother was in the toothpaste aisle of the Walmart in Rexburg, Idaho. As I was shopping, an enormously powerful feeling of love suddenly came over me. It wasn't just a general love. It was a distinct love for every person in that Walmart. It was physical in how overpowering it was. It felt like there wasn't enough of me to hold it all—like I was a cup and it was overflowing out of me because I wasn't big enough to contain it. I recognized that people were somewhere in the back of the store that I couldn't even see, but just knowing they were there, I felt an overwhelming, all-consuming love for them. As it was happening, a clear voice came into my mind: "What you are feeling is the smallest sliver of a fraction of the love your Heavenly Mother feels for all of Her children."

I walked around not knowing what to do with myself but not wanting the feeling to leave. After a while it did, but the experience changed me more than any other experience in my life. It taught me what I am supposed to be. It taught me how I am supposed to feel about other people. It taught me how I am supposed to resolve conflicts—that I am to always lead with love in every interaction. It taught me that the love our Heavenly Parents have for us is not passive but extremely active; it's everything to Them. It is Them.

Claire Easley

The Circle

The sculptor becomes the clay and the
clay becomes the sculptor as She
gives us life and we become
as Her —
it continues on and
on and on.

Olivia Flinders

"The anxiety and disquieting influence of this earth life could have been avoided had we stayed nestled in the household of our heavenly parents, but then how could we have progressed?"

President Barbara W. Winder, Relief Society general president, 1984-90[48]

I Found The Mother

I found The Mother
     in My Sisters

When my heart cried out
     desperate & searching
     I felt my answer
in the echoes

The echoes
     reverberating back
     from the hearts
of My Sisters

My Sisters
     who stand by me
     with a nod
       a word
         the pen

Our hands clasped
       arms stretched wide
       forming a search line
A safety net

We will comb
       this Earth together

She is there
       ... and She is here

We find The Mother
    in each other

We find The Mother
    Together

        Amber Kessinger

Peace

Ouch!
Why when I come here looking for peace do I
step on a rock?!
I'm exhausted, grieving and searching for peace,
all these beautifully manicured lawns
and I stand on the one rock??

Softly I hear Her whisper
"child, lift your foot"

I do so

Tears fall

As I pluck this "rock" from the ground
I see clearly its heart shape and the word
PEACE
engraved on it.

A treasure half buried
Waiting for me.

She sent me a tangible token
of Heaven sent PEACE

Not as the world gives, but as Jesus gives.

I hold PEACE,
knowing my Heavenly Mother hears me

Lorraine Pemberton

"And fundamentally, there is belief in a God who is over all the earth, and we are His children. As members of the Church of Jesus Christ, we understand that concept as well as anyone—that we are spiritual sons and daughters of heavenly parents, and that we have a divine nature. As such, we are brothers and sisters and have a responsibility and accountability to care for one another, and to look out for one another and to enable one another."

Sister Carol F. McConkie, counselor in Young Women general presidency, 2013-18[49]

Why

I am a person who needs to know the why. I simply cannot function in a pointless way. So, when I think about WHY I exist, it gives me not only peace but also a keen mechanism to prioritize my life when I realize my "highest aspiration" is to be like my Heavenly Parents.

McArthur Krishna

Welcome Home

A cycle, a pattern, a leap, a climb, traveling, journeying, tears, tiers, an earthly home, a heavenly home, houses, churches, temples; She is there. Welcome, Welcome, Welcome Home.

Pondering Heavenly Mother made me think about my heavenly homecoming.

I have long thought how wonderful it will be to hear the words,
"Well done my good and faithful servant" coming from my Heavenly Father.

And then, I thought, what would I like to hear from my Heavenly Mother?

The first thing that came to my mind was, "Welcome Home, baby girl."
The same greeting I give to my own daughters when they return to me now.
I'm over the moon, filled with joy to see them and hear their stories.

I thought of the flood of emotions that will accompany Her words and embrace, including a remembrance of my premortal childhood.

What do you hope your Heavenly Mother will say to you?

What do you imagine Her embrace to feel like?

Feel this now as you ponder.

Michelle Gessell

Reminiscing

I dream a lot about coming home.

Neal A. Maxwell spoke about our "regal homecoming" not being possible without "the anticipatory arrangements" of our Mother. But I imagine after the hubbub and celebration dies down, we'll have a good long chat about my trip away and I'll say

"Mom, do you remember when—"
and "Mom that part was hard"
and "Mom oh that part made it all worth it thank you"
and "Mom do you remember when I remembered you for the first time?"
And "Mom thank you for remembering me too"

And She'll laugh at how silly I sound

"Remember you? Dearest, you are engraved upon the palms of my hand and the marks of my womb,

your hopes and fears and joys and defeats and triumphs are continually before Me
I would cease to be God before I would cease to be Mother. I will never forsake you."

And I'll snuggle in close and we'll think about how similar we've become, how much I've grown like Her and I'll be glad and She'll be glad and our joy will be full.

Autumn Nelson

Invitation

I invite you to learn more about your divine potential. President Nelson has asked us to study, pray, and take time to listen to get divine guidance. As Alma 32:7 says, do an "experiment upon my words, and exercise a particle of faith." Do this experiment for yourself. Study, pray, and listen. There are hundreds of quotes, poems, articles, and artwork about Heavenly Mother for you to study. After a literature review, pray and listen. I believe you will have the same finding as me—more knowledge about your divine potential to be like our parents, Heavenly Mother and Heavenly Father. Our analysis, discussion, limitations, and future scope will all be different.

Restoring knowledge of our Heavenly Mother won't solve all of the world's problems. But I strongly believe this knowledge has power, and that power will bring much love and goodness into the world.

Darci Garcia

"Then shall they be gods, because they have no end; therefore shall they be from everlasting to everlasting, because they continue; then shall they be above all, because all things are subject unto them."

D&C 132:20

Before the Mother

My children teach me about myself
before the Mother.
My son, 4,
talks to his father
in the other room.
I don't want to grow big.
I only want to snuggle Mama
all of my days.
Days later he tells me,
I liked being a baby.
A pause.
It wasn't nice of you to stop
giving me baby milk.
I was hungry.
My baby, 1, climbs down
from off his chair
runs to me
if he sees me sit down,

snuggles on to my
soft lap.
My daughter, 6,
looks me firmly in the eyes
and says,
I want to be
You.

        Rachel Hunt Steenblik

CONCLUSION

A Celebration of Joy

"Joy is powerful, and focusing on **joy brings God's power** into our lives."

President Russell M. Nelson[50]

This is a Gospel of Joy

This is the Lord's restored church. This is the restored gospel. This gospel is a gospel of JOY. Joy in Christ—in His Atonement, in His promises, and in His and our Heavenly Parents' great love for us.

Ashli Carnicelli

Doctrine & Covenants 50:24

"That which is of God is light;"—the knowledge that our Mother in Heaven exists as a partner to our Father in Heaven is wonderful light!

"and [they] that receiveth light, and continueth in God,"—we accept this doctrine joyfully and follow the Savior to become more like Him and our Heavenly Parents.

"receiveth more light;"—we gain more and new revelation, we grow to be more empowered in living up to our privileges and divine potential.

"and that light groweth brighter and brighter"—Emma Smith said that the women of the Relief Society will do "extraordinary" things; we can gain further revelation and spiritual empowerment, becoming even more like the Savior and our Heavenly Parents.

"until the perfect day."—when we meet our Mother and Father and the Savior face to face and rejoice in our unity and love.

Trina Caudle

"When we return to our real home, it will be with the 'mutual approbation' of those who reign in the 'royal courts on high.' There we will find beauty such as mortal 'eye hath not seen'; we will hear sounds of surpassing music which mortal 'ear hath not heard.' Could such a regal homecoming be possible without the anticipatory arrangements of a Heavenly Mother?"

Elder Neal A. Maxwell[51]

Blessing to Believe, Nurture & Dream

~

Lindsey Larsen Myer

True and Lasting Happiness

~

For five years, I studied with Lama Migmar, Tibetan Lama and Buddhist Chaplain at Harvard University. He taught me about two types of happiness in the world. One type, *samsara*, is a fleeting worldly happiness that comes from short term experiences such as eating ice cream or receiving an award. *Samadhi*, also known as *Nirvana*, is a deep abiding happiness that is untouched by external circumstances.

This joy is untouched by external circumstances. THIS is the joy of our gospel, of Christ, of Heavenly Mother and Father. This "plan of happiness" is not a "plan of samsara." It's a plan of Samadhi. This happiness is the deep and abiding love of Christ.

The trials and thorny patches of mortality will come. They are guaranteed. The joy of knowing that we are deeply, infinitely loved by a perfect Christ and our perfect Father and Mother in Heaven is an untouchable joy—it does not diminish, come what may. We are Theirs. We are loved. And as we are headed toward returning to Them, we know our joy will be eternal.

Ashli Carnicelli

Carrying

We walk together
She and I,
my head nodding
against Her chest
Her feet on the ground
carrying us
Both.

Rachel Hunt Steenblik

The Seed of Faith

~

Alma invites us to experiment upon the word—the words of the gospel—by comparing it to a seed. He said, "If ye give place that a seed may be planted in your heart, behold, if it be a true seed, or a good seed, if ye do not cast it out by your unbelief, that ye will resist the Spirit of the Lord, behold, it will begin to swell within your breasts." If it is a good seed—if the word is true and good—it will begin to enlarge your soul and enlighten your understanding, and it will be delicious to you (Alma 32:28).

Can you "give place" to plant the truths we know about our Heavenly Mother in your heart? Have you felt your faith begin to grow, begin to swell and enlighten and enlarge your soul?

We may not have a "perfect knowledge" of Heavenly Mother, but we can nourish the truths that we do have "with great care, that it may get root, that it may grow up, and bring forth fruit unto us" (Alma 32:37).

What fruits have come to you from developing a testimony of Heavenly Mother? How can you nourish the word that you have planted in your heart through faith, diligence, and patience to eventually taste the sweetness and joy of the "fruit of the tree of life"? (Alma 32:40–41).

Aspen Moore

What to Remember

She moves
and the earth trembles
She groans
and the life births
She thinks
and we all exist

Olivia Flinders

Clues

Read your Patriarchal blessing searching for clues of Heavenly Mother. This list of words can help you look for symbolism:

parents, mother, motherhood, wisdom, understanding, counsel, Throne of God, happiness, blessed, fear of the Lord, reverence, anointed, oil, heavenly light, the Spirit of God, fruitful, fertility, tree of life, living water, temple, ancestors, posterity, blood, progress, Zion, rebirth, weaving, heart, virtue, divine, delight, bread and wine, the Love of God.

If you don't have a patriarchal blessing, sit in silence to ponder and write what you feel Heavenly Mother would want you to know about your path in life, your struggles, and eternal destiny.

Kate Gregory

Evergreen

Each year in preparation for Christmas we bring a tree inside our homes. When I look at that evergreen tree, I think of the love of Heavenly Mother filling my home as it reaches upward. She, with the Father, gave Her Son. The Savior's love in giving His life reflects Their great love—a love that, like the evergreen tree, will not fade or fall away when the cold winds of life come. His love and Her love are enduring, giving everlasting life to my heart.

Angela Ricks

Diversity

Our Heavenly Parents must love diversity because diversity is the way our world has been created, and the people on it. If our Heavenly Parents love meadows, forests, ocean life, and rainbows, what can we do when we feel an urge to stay comfortable by surrounding ourselves with people who look, think, and act like us? How can we embrace and celebrate our Heavenly Parents' diversity around us?

Becky Edwards

Mirror Meditation

I meditate often about Mother Eve, Mother Mary, and Mother Earth—all stewards over sacred and holy callings. Each tasked with bringing pieces of heaven to our hearts and hands. The depth of their individual and collective sacrifice is magnanimous and provides for generations upon generations. I honor them for their perpetuation of progress and sanctification of living things. When I reflect inwards, I am encouraged to reach outwards and seek sisterhood, to celebrate the diverse and on-going "mothers" in our lives—the varied caregivers of our souls and bodies. My heart whispers that there is much to learn from each of them as they are Womanhood Incarnate. For all these beings are but echoes of The Divine Feminine.

Tasha Antoniak

Affirmation

No matter who you are, you come from Love. You are spiritually begotten from a long celestial lineage of love. There are more souls out there filled to the brim of their being with love for you than exist people who have ever lived on this earth. Father, Mother, Brother, on and on forever. This is your ancestral inheritance.

Autumn Nelson

"I have heard it said by some that the reason women in the Church struggle to know themselves is because they don't have a divine female role model. But we do. We believe we have a mother in heaven. . . . Furthermore, I believe we know much more about our eternal nature than we think we do; and it is our sacred obligation to express our knowledge, to teach it to our young sisters and daughters, and in so doing to strengthen their faith and help them."

Sister Patricia Holland, counselor in Young Women general presidency, 1984-86[52]

Joy

I love the imagery of all of nature celebrating. Isaiah 55:12 describes what happens when people make a covenant with God: "For ye shall go out with joy, and be led forth with peace: the mountains and the hills shall break forth before you into singing, and all the trees of the field shall clap *their* hands." Isn't that marvelous? Let's celebrate the joy of knowing we have a Mother in Heaven.

McArthur Krishna

Making Up For Lost Time

Will the Father braid my hair
And the Mother tell me stories

Will They sing to me Their lullabies
And share with me Their glory

Will They clothe me in the stars
And accept Christ's offering fully

Will They be pleased by my heart
And welcome me into Their holiest of holies
They are—waiting
Welcoming me home
Mother, Father
Calling out "our daughter"
They are—waiting
Guiding me home to Them.

Ashley Lauren Workman

Divine Feminine

Carly White

Heavenly Mother

To describe
the indescribable
To weave
Our Holy Mother
with words
seems laughable
Yet—
with bated breath
and open hearts
and wetted eyes
We yearn.
We call for Her
Like a mother
about to be delivered
of her child
Reaching upward
and crying out
for this Mother—this
Holy of Holies.
So press on we must

with our words
and impressions
and brilliant imaginings
of who She is
and whom She might be.
This sacred feminine
Deity
Source of our source
Love of our love
Deepest of our depths
(which is why She's just so unnerving)
the nourishing
the below the surface
and then below that
and below that still
Until we think
We will cease to exist, but instead find ourselves
    there.
She is the raging fire
We fear we cannot contain

(and we can't)
the fire that burns to ashes
All in its path
with the power it gives
to build anew—
Better
More Holy
More pure
More, *more*.
She is the love that knows no bounds
the love that never stops reaching
like the endless sea
stretching its long fingers
into rivers
that it may just touch us.
She is in the tender height
of the lover's embrace
as we give and receive
as our love conceives
and life begins anew

and anew
and anew
Until we see the echoes of Her sweet face
everywhere we go
in the heart of every woman
everywhere
She is there.
As the babe in the womb,
we are within Her
to such that
we cannot discern
where She ends
and we begin
our separateness
never fully realized
She is the air we breathe

Until one day
like a bolt
We will race towards the Light
and meet Her embrace
as we did on this side of the veil
with our earthly mothers
and the joyful recognition of Her
will be as a mirror—
She was there all along.

        Ashli Carnicelli

Contributors

> "Within the Church of Jesus Christ of Latter-day Saints, women have been a crucial part of one another's lives—spiritually, emotionally, intellectually, socially."
>
> Jill Mulvay Derr,
> Church historian[53]

We deeply appreciate the beautiful contributions of so many wonderful people, sharing your wisdom and reflections about our Heavenly Mother. Your grace, dignity, and power have become a crucial part of our lives.

Ashli, Trina, and McArthur

Sarah Adamson
Camilla Alves
Krystal Root Andrew
Tasha Antoniak
Paige Atwood
Moriann Barker
Krystal Richey Barnes
Shima Baughman
Kirsten Beitler
Alison Bennett
Arawn Billings
Kristina A. Bishoff
Jaylen Dodds Bohman
Alice Bradford Brown
Jared Buhler
Jessica Burdette
Isla Rose Carnicelli
McCall Char
Hanna Choi
DeAnna Christensen
Anne Clark
Lindsay Collingwood
Lee Correia
Rebecca Cromar
Brittany Cromar
Natalie Cosby
Becky Curtis
Maddie Daetwyler

Rose Datoc Dall
Allison Dayton
Brittany Deltoro
Laura Detweiler
Charity DuFort
Claire Easley
Chelsea Echols
Becky Edwards
Blakelee Ellis
Laura Erekson
Marie-Françoise Euvrard
Olivia Flinders
Rowan Li Forsyth
Eva J. Frost
Tracie Frost
Sage Gallagher
Darci Garcia
Christie Gardiner
Minta Garvin
Megan Geilman
Beccah Gerber
Michelle Gessell
Kayla Gisseman
April Green
Kelli Green
Mandy Green
Anne Gregerson
Kate Gregory

Contributors

Julie de Azevedo Hanks
Sadie Hanna
Kristine Hoyt
Erin Hulme
Channing Olivia Hyde
Amanda Jenkins
Katie Jordan
Amber Kessinger
Zara Krishna
Amanda Landeen
Dylan Landeen
Jolyn Laney
Amber Lanning
Lorren Lemmons
Jennie Loomis
Lauren Madsen
Britt Manjarrez
Kate McArthur
Hannah Milmont McCourt
Emily Christensen McPhie
Kristin Miller
Aspen Moore
Kerstin Z. Moore
Lindsey Larsen Myer
Autumn Nelson
Cassia Nielsen
Nancy Andruk Olson
Lisa Page
Jessie Payne
Lorraine Pemberton
Eliza Peterson
Angela Ricks
Emily Roundy
Kate Ryskamp
Anita Schley
Alynne Scirkovich
Mindy Sebastian
Andrea Sloop
Bethany Brady Spalding
Rachel Hunt Steenblik
Lydia Theobald
Tammy Zufelt Thomas
Michal Thomas
Megan Thompson
Mindy Thompson
Jessica Vergara
Malinda Wagstaff
Megan Watson
Char Weiler
Madeleine Wells
Carly White
Alyssa Wilkinson
Jessica Woodbury
Ashley Lauren Workman
Bonnie Young
Rebecca Young

"Rejoice in the diversity of our sisterhood! It is the diversity of colors in a spectrum that makes a rainbow. It is the diversity in our circumstances that gives us compassionate hearts. It is the diversity of our spiritual gifts that benefits the Church."

Sister Chieko N. Okazaki
counselor in Relief Society
general presidency, 1990-97[54]

ASHLI CARNICELLI graduated from The Boston Conservatory with a bachelor's degree in music, vocal performance. She is a convert to the Church from her Catholic upbringing in Boston. Ashli writes a bi-monthly newsletter bearing her testimony of Christ called "The Pearls." The fulness of the gospel (especially the temple!) brings her lasting and deep joy. She and her husband Tony are the parents of four daughters and reside in Charleston, South Carolina.

TRINA CAUDLE is an editor, writer, and reader focused on personal stories. She graduated from Western Oregon University with a bachelor's degree in history and journalism, is the Interview Editor for the LDS Women Project, and provides editing services for authors. She is a life-long Latter-day Saint and believes that the gathering of Israel should be done gently, with baked goods in one hand and nothing in the other so she can give you a hug. Trina and her family live in the Washington DC metro area.

McARTHUR KRISHNA graduated from BYU with both an undergraduate and masters degree. She co-owned an award-winning ideas marketing firm for a decade until she retired, got married, and moved to India. With church a plane ride away, she started spending home church time researching and writing children's books. Over eight years she published 17 books, six with Deseret Book. Along the way, she has been called in to discuss women's issues in the church with the General Women's Outreach Committee at church headquarters, had art from her *Girls Who Choose God* books hung in the Conference Center for two years, and had one of her own art pieces selected for the Church's International Art competition. The art from her book "*Our Heavenly Family, our Earthly Families*" was the first art portraying Heavenly Mother published at Deseret Book. After its release, the Church purchased a 12' × 8' piece for their permanent collection—and it currently hangs at the Church History Museum on Temple Square. As you can see, McArthur believes in being a "doer" of the Word.

References

1. President Russell M. Nelson, "Come Follow Me," April 2019 general conference.

2. Carole M. Stephens, "Do We Know What We Have?" October 2013 general conference.

3. Bonnie H. Cordon, "Beloved Daughters," October 2019 general conference.

4. Elder Rudger Clawson, "Our Mother in Heaven," *Millennial Star* 72 (September 29, 1910): 619-20.

5. Jeffrey R. Holland, "The Laborers in the Vineyard," April 2012 general conference.

6. M. Russell Ballard, "Return and Receive," April 2017 general conference.

7. First Presidency, "The Origin and Destiny of Man," *Improvement Era* 12 (November 1909): 78. First Presidency: Joseph F. Smith, John R. Winder, Anthon H. Lund.

8. Julie B. Beck, "You Have a Noble Birthright," April 2006 general conference.

9. M. Russell Ballard, "Answer to Life's Questions," April 1995 general conference.

10. Dieter F. Uchtdorf, "O How Great The Plan of Our God," October 2016 general conference.

11. Sharon Eubank, "This is A Woman's Church," FAIR Conference, Provo UT, August 8, 2014.

12. Dale G. Renlund, "Your Divine Nature and Eternal Destiny," April 2022 general conference.

13. Susa Young Gates, "History of the Young Ladies' Mutual Improvement Association of the Church of Jesus Christ of Latter-Day Saints," *Deseret News* (1911), p. 16 footnote.

14. Elder Rudger Clawson, "Our Mother in Heaven," *Latter-day Saints Millennial Star* 72, (September 29, 1910), p. 619-20.

15. Orson F. Whitney, Conference Report April 1929, p. 110. Quoted in Spencer W. Kimball, *Faith Precedes the Miracle* (Salt Lake City: Deseret Book, 1972), p. 98.

16. Ardeth G. Kapp, "A Time for Hope," October 1986 general conference.

17. Barbara B. Smith, "A Season for Strength," October 1983 general conference.

18. Gordon B. Hinckley, "Daughters of God," October 1991 general conference.

19. Eliza R. Snow, 1804-1887. This poem was first titled "My Father in Heaven," and published in the *Times and Seasons* newspaper in Nauvoo, Illinois in October 1845. It was published as a

Latter-day Saint hymn in 1851. The words to this poem are in the public domain.

20. James E. Talmage, "The Philosophical Basis of 'Mormonism'," *Improvement Era* 18 (September 1915): 950.

21. Russell M. Nelson, "Revelation for the Church, Revelation for Our Lives," April 2018 general conference.

22. Elder Ulisses Soares, "In Partnership With the Lord," October 2022 general conference.

23. Susa Young Gates, "The Vision Beautiful," *Improvement Era* 23 (April 1920), p. 542.

24. "That is a startling doctrine, I recognize, to some folk, and yet we ought to be governed by reason in giving consideration to this doctrine which is a revelation from God." Elder Melvin J. Ballard. Bryant S. Hinckley, *Sermons and Mission Services of Melvin Joseph Ballard*, (Salt Lake City: Deseret Book, 1949), p. 205.

25. Bryant S. Hinckley, *Sermons and Mission Services of Melvin Joseph Ballard*, (Salt Lake City: Deseret Book, 1949), 205.

26. Russell M. Nelson, "Thou Shalt Have No Other Gods," April 1996 general conference.

27. Vaughn J. Featherstone, "A Champion of Youth," October 1987 general conference.

28. Susan L. Warner, "Remember How Thou Hast Received and Heard," April 1996 general conference.

29. Jeffrey R. Holland, "Behold Thy Mother," October 2015 general conference.

30. Reyna I. Aburto, "With One Accord," April 2018 general conference.

31. Jane B. Bingham, "United in Accomplishing God's Work," April 2020 general conference.

32. James E. Talmage, "Services at the Tabernacle," *Deseret News*, April 29, 1902: p. 13.

33. Chieko N. Okazaki, "Rowing Your Boat," October 1994 general conference.

34. Patricia Holland, "Filling the Measure of Your Creation," BYU devotional, Provo UT, January 17, 1989.

35. Jean B. Bingham, "How Vast is Our Purpose," BYU Women's Conference, Provo UT, May 5, 2017.

36. Larry M. Gibson, "Following Heavenly Father's Plan," BYU devotional, Provo UT, March 2014.

37. Jeffrey R. Holland, "Belonging: A View of Membership," *Ensign*, April 1980.

38. Dieter F. Uchtdorf, "A Yearning for Home," October 2017 general conference.

39. Chieko N. Okazaki, *Sanctuary*, (Salt Lake City: Deseret Book, 1997), 129-130.

40. Russell M. Nelson, "Perfection Pending," October 1995 general conference.

41. Ulisses Soares, "Abide in the Lord's Territory," April 2012 general conference.

42. Elaine L. Jack, "Identity of a Young Woman," October 1989 general conference.

43. Jean B. Bingham, "Endowed with Priesthood Power," BYU Women's Conference, Provo UT, May 2, 2019.

44. David Steindl-Rast, "Gratitude," May 4, 2021, YouTube.

45. Linda K. Burton, "Certain Women," April 2017 general conference.

46. Spencer W. Kimball, "Privileges and Responsibilities of Sisters," October 1978 general conference.

47. Glenn L. Pace, "The Divine Nature and Destiny of Women," BYU devotional, Provo UT, March 9, 2010.

48. Barbara W. Winder, "Hope in Christ," October 1986 general conference.

49. "Sister Carol F. McConkie on building bridges through service, advocacy and education." Host Sarah Jane Weaver, *Church News* podcast, May 31, 2022. Episode 86, 40:28.

50. Russell M. Nelson, "Joy and Spiritual Survival," October 2016 general conference.

51. Neal A. Maxwell, "The Women of God," April 1978 general conference.

52. Patricia T. Holland, "One Thing Needful," *Ensign*, October 1987.

53. Jill Mulvay Derr, "Strength in Our Union: The Making of Mormon Sisterhood," in *Sisters in Spirit: Mormon Women in Historical and Cultural Perspective*, (Urbana: University of Illinois Press, 1987), p. 154-5.

54. Chieko Okasaki, "Rejoice in Every Good Thing," October 1991 general conference.